UNIVERSITY OF STRATHCLYDE
30125 00737589 1

D1147814

Acquiring, Developing, and Implementing Accounting Information Systems

Ulric J. Gelinas, Jr.
Bentley College

Steve G. Sutton
University of Connecticut

James E. Hunton
Bentley College

ANDERSONIAN LIBRARY
★
WITHDRAWN
FROM
LIBRARY
STOCK
★
UNIVERSITY OF STRATHCLYDE

THOMSON
＊
SOUTH-WESTERN

Australia · Canada · Mexico · Singapore · Spain · United Kingdom · United States

THOMSON

SOUTH-WESTERN

Acquiring, Developing, and Implementing Accounting Information Systems, 6e
Ulric J. Gelinas, Jr., Steve G. Sutton, and James E. Hunton

VP/Editorial Director:
Jack W. Calhoun

VP/Editor-in-Chief:
George Werthman

Publisher:
Rob Dewey

Acquisitions Editor:
Sharon Oblinger

Developmental Editor:
Carol Bennett

Marketing Manager:
Chip Kislack

Production Editor:
Chris Sears

Manufacturing Coordinator:
Doug Wilke

Technology Project Editor:
Amy Wilson

Media Editor:
Kelly Reid

Design Project Manager:
Bethany Casey

Production House:
Cover to Cover Publishing, Inc.

Cover Designer:
Bethany Casey

Cover Images:
© Getty Images, Inc.
Photographer: Jason Reed

Internal Designer:
Bethany Casey

Printer:
WestGroup
Eagan, MN

COPYRIGHT © 2005
by South-Western, part of the Thomson Corporation. South-Western, Thomson, and the Thomson logo are trademarks used herein under license.

Printed in the United States of America
1 2 3 4 5 07 06 05 04

Package ISBN: 0-324-22106-1
Book Only ISBN: 0-324-23359-0
CD ISBN: 0-324-23360-4

Library of Congress Control Number: 2004106584

ALL RIGHTS RESERVED.

No part of this work covered by the copyright hereon may be reproduced or used in any form or by any means—graphic, electronic, or mechanical, including photocopying, recording, taping, Web distribution or information storage and retrieval systems—without the written permission of the publisher.

For permission to use material from this text or product, submit a request online at http://www.thomsonrights.com. Any additional questions about permissions can be submitted by email to thomsonrights@thomson.com.

For more information contact South-Western, 5191 Natorp Boulevard, Mason, Ohio, 45040. Or you can visit our Internet site at: http://www.swlearning.com

UNIVERSITY OF STRATHCLYDE
23 AUG 2004
UNIVERSITY LIBRARY

D
657·0285
GEL

Preface

In this supplemental text the journey through the field of accounting information systems (AIS) continues. In the main text some background was given related to AIS, such as enterprise systems and e-Business. Then, the many parts of the AIS wheel were explored. For example, depending on how your AIS course was designed, database management systems and the design of relational databases may have been explored. Also, one or more chapters on enterprise risk management may have been covered. Finally, we hope that you have had an opportunity to study several of the business processes described in Chapters 10 through 16 of the text.

This supplement describes the processes organizations perform to select the software and hardware they will use to enable their business processes and related information systems. In any accounting career path, you will need to be aware of, and indeed skilled in, the processes described in this supplement. This preface provides an overview of this supplement, descriptions of each chapter and *The Accounting Library* software that accompanies this supplement, suggestions on ways the supplement can be used to complement the use of the main text, and a conclusion with a summary on the importance of developing knowledge and skills related to the systems development process.

OVERVIEW OF THIS SUPPLEMENT

In four comprehensive chapters, this supplement to *Accounting Information Systems* provides an extensive overview of the selection of accounting information systems—including the important buy-versus-build decision. Issues considered in selecting the right "off-the-shelf" software, including ERP software, or developing software internally are examined. The supplement acts as a guide through the systematic steps that should be taken in order to decide whether to modify purchased software, to adjust business processes to mesh with the software, or to build information systems that support existing business processes. Chapter S1 examines the key steps undertaken when software will be purchased. Chapter S2 reviews the systems analysis phase of systems development, with an emphasis on software that will be developed internally. Chapters S3 and S4 complete the detailed review of the development process by describing the hardware selection and detailed design (Chapter S3) and implementation (Chapter S4), that must be undertaken whether software is acquired or developed in-house.

CHAPTER-BY-CHAPTER

Chapter S1 gives a brief overview of the entire systems development life cycle for the situation in which software will be purchased. Topics include a discussion of the external sources of AIS software, how the accountant would be involved in the AIS acquisition process, determining the requirements for the new AIS, and developing specifications for the new AIS that will satisfy those requirements. Finally, the chapter concludes by describing a process for identifying and selecting AIS software using *The Accounting Library*, the software included with this supplement.

Chapter S2 provides an overview of the entire systems development life cycle for the situation in which the software will be developed in-house. While this chapter may seem to go over the same ground as Chapter S1, the discussions are focused on the tasks that must be completed when the choice is to develop systems in-house. The chapter then provides detailed coverage of the first phase of systems development, the analysis phase. This provides a detailed coverage of the development of systems specifications for systems to be developed in-house. This chapter also covers topics—such as quality assurance, project management, and change management—that are relevant to either the make or buy alternative to systems development.

Chapter S3 covers selecting hardware (for purchased software or software developed in-house) and detailed design (most of which is needed for either purchase or in-house development). Topics include alternative sources for computer hardware; evaluation of vendor proposals; and design of databases, forms, and conversion routines.

Chapter S4 covers systems implementation (again, most is needed in either the purchase or the build situation). Topics include approaches to implementation and acquiring, testing, and installing the new system. The chapter concludes with consideration of the issues that follow a system implementation, such as the post-implementation review and systems maintenance.

THE ACCOUNTING LIBRARY

A fully working version of *The Accounting Library*, a software system designed specifically to assist organizations in identifying externally available software with the best fit for their organization, is included on the CD-ROM with this text. This wonderful tool helps in the understanding of the key concepts underlying software selection all the way from large ERP software packages to smaller accounting packages for family businesses. While using the software, an understanding is gained of the key issues that should be considered during the systems survey and systems analysis stages of the systems development life cycle, for either the build or buy situation. In short, a user can learn about selecting pre-packaged software versus building a system, and then progress on through the life cycle to understand all of the steps in modifying pre-packaged systems and/or building systems tailored to the organization.

HOW TO USE THIS SUPPLEMENT

The supplement can be used as the central focus of the AIS or Advanced AIS course or as a special topic within one of the other approaches to the AIS courses (see Figure P.2 on page xi of the text). If the AIS course is to focus on this supplement, the following is recommended:

- First, as with any approach to the AIS course, it is necessary to read Chapters 1 through 3 of the text to get a background in AIS.
- Next, studying Chapter 4 of the text, Documenting Information Systems is recommended. To be able to document the future design of a business process, learning to read and to prepare data flow diagrams (DFDs) and systems flowcharts is necessary.
- Then, Chapters 5 and 6 in the text should be studied to learn about database management systems and relational databases. This will provide the skills to design the database for a new system and will complement skills in documenting the design of the processes that were learned in Chapter 4 of the text.
- At this point in the course studying the chapters in this supplement should begin.
- As the study of this supplement continues, one or more of the enterprise risk management chapters could be covered (Chapters 7 through 9 in the text). For example, Chapters 7 and 9 in the text give the ability to analyze the control features in a present or proposed AIS.

- Finally, one or more business processes could be covered (Chapters 10 through 16 of the text). This would provide a context for systems development. For example, you could learn about the organizational context, management decision making, and controls that are typical to a business process. As a minimum, the business process chapters are a good reference for key features and controls in the business process that is the subject of your development.

If this supplement is to be a topic within the AIS course using one of the other approaches to the AIS course (see Figure P.2 on page xi of the text), then one or more chapters of this supplement may be covered at any time after about the mid-point in the course. For example, Chapter S1 and *The Accounting Library* software could be used with any of the business process chapters (Chapters 10 through 16 of the text) to analyze the requirements for a business process and to obtain a list of software products that would enable those requirements.

With either of these general approaches—systems development as the focus or as a complementary topic—a term project is provided with the AIS text. This project is provided at the text Web site http://gelinas.swlearning.com. This project has been used with great success over the years to give students an opportunity to use the tools in the text and supplement in a real-life setting and to analyze a real business process and make recommendations for improving that process.

SUMMARY

The processes described in this supplement are important for any accounting career path. Indeed, for some career paths, knowledge and skills related to systems development may determine success! Table S1.2 on page 9 enumerates many typical accounting jobs and the systems development related functions performed by those holding those positions. Let's review a few of these here.

Within an organization you might be a staff accountant, controller, or reporting officer (i.e., business, financial, managerial reporting). As such you may be the "business process owner" for the AIS system that will be acquired or developed in-house (i.e., the user, purchaser, or implementer in Table S1.2). In these cases you will need to ensure that the new system will meet your business needs, that there are controls in place to ensure that the system operates reliably, that data is accurate, complete, and valid, etc.

You also may have chosen a career path that has led you to be a consultant and/or systems specialist (i.e., analyst or consultant in Table S1.2). In these cases you will need to be able to perform the processes described in this supplement to ensure that the systems development process is performed correctly and efficiently and that the new system does indeed meet user needs.

Finally, another career path might lead you to be an auditor (i.e., internal auditor or external auditor in Table S1.2). As you can see in Table S1.2 it may have been the auditors' recommendations that led to the present development effort. Or, the auditor may participate in the development process to ensure that the process follows prescribed procedures and that the new system has adequate controls and is auditable.

This has been a very brief overview of the importance of skills related to system development. Certainly, many additional situations will occur for which applying the material in this supplement will come to the forefront. To give some idea of the skills that might be required, a review of Table P.1 on pages xiii–xvi in the main text may be needed to see the number of skills prescribed for professional accountants that are covered in this supplement.

We hope you enjoy continuing the journey through AIS. We believe that the material in this supplement will help in developing some skills that will be central to success in the accounting profession.

Contents

S1 AIS Acquisition Cycle   1

Synopsis   2

Introduction   3

Acquiring an AIS from External Parties   5

Accountants Involvement in AIS Acquisition   6

Achieving AIS Acquisition Objectives   10

Project Management   11

AIS Analysis   12

Conduct Preliminary Survey   12

Perform Needs Analysis   17

AIS Selection   24

Evaluate Feasible Solutions   24

Determine Final Solution   27

AIS Implementation and Operation   29

Summary   29

Review Questions   30

Discussion Questions   31

Problems   31

Key Terms   33

S2 Structured Systems Analysis   34

Synopsis   35

Introduction   35

Controlling the Systems Development Process   36

Quality Assurance   36

Systems Development Methodology   37

Business Process Reengineering   40

Change Management   42

Accountant's Involvement in Systems Development 44

Systems Survey   44

Systems Survey Definition and Goals   45

Systems Survey Tasks and Documents   45

Structured Systems Analysis   47

Systems Analysis Definition and Goals   47

Systems Analysis Tasks and Documents   48

Summary   61

Review Questions   62

Discussion Questions   62
Problems   64
Key Terms   68

S3 Systems Selection and Design   69
Synopsis   70
Introduction to Systems Selection   70
The Accountant's Involvement in Systems Selection   72
The Systems Selection Deliverable:
    The Approved Configuration Plan   73
Triggering Systems Selection   73
Hardware Acquisition Alternatives   74
Internal Acquisition   74
External Acquisition   74
Financing Alternatives   75
The Intermediate Steps in Systems Selection   76
Prepare Requests for Proposal   77
Evaluate Vendor Proposals   78
Assess Software Plan   83
Complete Configuration Plan   86
Introduction to Systems Design   87
Definition and Goals   87
Systems Design Tasks   89
The Accountant's Involvement in Systems Design   89
The Systems Design Deliverable: The
    Approved Systems Design Document   89
Triggering Systems Design   91
The Intermediate Steps in Systems Design   91
Specify Modules   91
Develop Implementation Plan and Budget   92
Develop Implementation Test Plan   92
Develop User Manual   92
Develop Training Program   92
Complete Systems Design Document   93
Summary   93
Review Questions   95
Discussion Questions   95
Problems   96
Key Terms   100

S4 Systems Implementation and Operation   101
Synopsis   102
Introduction   102

Introduction to Systems Implementation   104
Approaches to Implementation   104
Systems Implementation Plans   106
**The Accountant's Involvement
in Systems Implementation   106**
**The Systems Implementation Deliverable:
The Project Completion Report   109**
Triggering Systems Implementation   109
**The Intermediate Steps in
Systems Implementation   110**
Complete the Design   110
Acquire Hardware and Software   110
Write, Test, Debug, and Document
Computer Programs   111
Select, Train, and Educate Personnel   112
Complete User Manual   113
Test System   113
Obtain Approvals   115
Conduct Conversion   115
Systems Operation   116
The Post-Implementation Review   116
Systems Maintenance   119
Summary   121
Review Questions   124
Discussion Questions   125
Problems   125
Key Terms   132

Glossary   133

Index   136

chapter
S1

Learning Objectives

- To describe and employ a structured approach to acquiring an AIS.
- To understand the nature and scope of accountants' involvement when acquiring an AIS.
- To be able to select an AIS that is aligned with the organization's objectives.
- To appreciate the importance of conducting proper and thorough AIS needs assessments.
- To use a needs analysis program, called *The Accounting Library*, to help narrow down the potential set of AIS solutions.
- To select a final AIS solution from among competing alternatives.
- To recognize that the best AIS can fail if the implementation is flawed.

AIS Acquisition Cycle

FoxMeyer Drug, a $5 billion company and leading distributor of pharmaceuticals, decided to upgrade its warehouse and distribution system, as the old Unisys mainframe system was crumbling under the intense load of processing nearly 500,000 sales orders each day. As explained by a former executive with FoxMeyer, "Shipping pharmaceuticals isn't like shipping bananas. There are a lot of government controls and procedures in different states. Many drugs are heavily secured. Some quickly expire. Meanwhile, hospitals need a steady flow of these drugs, because they're literally dealing with life and death. You can't make arbitrary or late shipments." After searching for a software vendor who could handle FoxMeyer's needs, management decided to purchase an ERP system from SAP. Implementing an ERP system is risky under the best of circumstances due to the inordinate number of complexities involved. Unfortunately, this $100 million investment turned into a nightmare: Millions of dollars of distribution orders were misdirected, many orders were completely omitted from picking and shipping manifests, and some orders were sent out multiple times and many customers were lost to competitors. The bottom line was that FoxMeyer Drug filed for bankruptcy and sued SAP, among other parties, for its collapse. The suit claimed that SAP's gross negligence was a significant factor in the drug company's business failure. Among many allegations, FoxMeyer asserted that it could connect only 6 of its 23 warehouses nearly one year after signing with SAP, the SAP software was capable of processing only 10,000 orders per day rather than the required 500,000 orders, and the company lost a potential $1 billion per year due to implementation problems. A footnote to SAP's 2002 annual report reads (in part): ". . . The discovery phase of the litigation is proceeding. While the ultimate outcome of this matter cannot be presently determined with certainty, the Company [SAP] believes that FoxMeyer's claims in this action are without merit. The Company is vigorously defending against the claims. . . ." What went wrong? Among many contributing factors were:

- FoxMeyer selected an ERP system that could not process their daily volume of orders.
- During the SAP implementation period, FoxMeyer was also attempting to install a robotic order picking system in its warehouses, which would dramatically speed up and improve the accuracy of order processing.
- Management was aggressively pursuing a $1 billion per year contract with a prospective client based on

prices that depended on the successful implementation of SAP *and* the new warehouse system.

- Management constantly changed its expectations—effectively increasing the scope of the project as it unfolded.

- Management kept pressuring the implementation team to speed up, while simultaneously demanding more out of the system.

As an accountant, you will undoubtedly be involved with modifying, analyzing, selecting, implementing, and/or using an AIS. In any of these roles, you will want to do all you can to avoid the tragedy that struck FoxMeyer. In this chapter we will examine a structured approach to acquiring an AIS from an external vendor with the aim of minimizing the risk of implementation failure.

SYNOPSIS

Driven by a host of sometimes complementary, but often conflicting, demands, the selection of accounting information systems (AIS) and other information systems throughout organizations requires considerable forethought, as constraints, tradeoffs, and tough decisions exist at every turn in the road. For instance, users are demanding more robust services from their information systems, customers are insisting on quicker response times and more flexible interfaces, organizations are becoming more internally interconnected, trading partners are moving toward fully integrated supply chains, competitive business pressures are bearing down on today's organizations, and new opportunities provided by advanced information technologies are cropping up everywhere. As a result, the modern organization must adapt its information systems quickly and continuously. The tentacles of AIS reach quite deep into most other information systems throughout the organization; as such, AIS must continuously adjust to rapidly changing conditions. Examples of how demand pressures can manifest themselves in AIS adaptations include:

- Users throughout the organization are demanding added functionality and increased access to the AIS. For example, salespersons need access to customer and inventory data while away from the office.

- Customers want better service, as measured by flexibility, speed, quality, and availability (24 hours a day, 7 days a week, called 24/7). For instance, customers might be granted limited access to the AIS to order goods, check shipments, or pay their bills online—anywhere and anytime.

ENTERPRISE SYSTEMS
- Management decides to implement an enterprise system to facilitate the interconnectivity of business processes and improve overall internal control throughout the organization. Many times, such implementations first require *reengineering* of the existing business and information processes. Then, the organization must select a system that is most compatible with the newly designed processes, which has vast implications for the AIS.

E-BUSINESS
- To reduce costs and provide better service, many organizations are utilizing the power of advanced information technology to create virtual *supply chain* integration with trading partners. Such integration often requires dramatic changes to business models, IT infrastructures, and AIS processes.

- Driven by competition and technological advances, organizations are embedding Internet, wireless, and other technologies deeper than ever before into their organizational processes. As such, Web-enabled and wireless functionalities are must-have features for some organizations when selecting an AIS.

- The metrics for making important decisions are collected and analyzed in the AIS. For example, measures of profitability of customers and products, the efficiency of production functions, and the performance of vendors all depend, partly, on data in the AIS.

When acquiring an AIS, system functionality must be properly aligned with the organization's strategies and objectives. In this chapter, you will learn how to acquire an AIS solution (meaning, accounting software) from an external vendor in a methodical and controlled fashion, for a structured approach will best ensure ultimate success. In doing so, we will discuss the issues and procedures involved in conducting a preliminary survey, performing a needs analysis, evaluating alternative solutions, and purchasing an AIS from an external vendor. In Chapters S2 through S4 we will cover the entire process, in somewhat more detail, with emphasis on developing the AIS solution in-house.

CONTROLS

As an accountant, you are uniquely qualified to participate, and even lead, this process. As an information management and business measurement professional, you will bring to the table important knowledge and skills, including knowledge of the business processes and the business context for the new AIS, expertise in internal controls that will be so important during the development process and for the new system, and skills with metrics that will be needed to make important decisions and to monitor the acquisition process.

INTRODUCTION

Organizations not wishing to or unable to develop software in-house may purchase, rent, or lease a commercially available software package. Some organizations have rented software packages and used them to benchmark software being developed in-house. The rented software may also provide an interim solution while a system is developed in-house and might be retained on a long-term basis if it proves to be superior to the in-house solution.

Software can be acquired from computer manufacturers, software vendors, mail-order houses and retail stores (for microcomputer software), turnkey system suppliers, service bureaus, systems integrators, outsourcing firms, and application service providers.

A **turnkey system** is a system in which a supplier has purchased computer hardware and has developed or acquired software to put together a computer system to be sold to end users. These systems are sold to firms needing a specialized system, such as newspaper editing and typesetting, or to firms preferring to transfer their development responsibilities to the turnkey supplier. When users receive a turnkey system, they need only to "turn the key" to begin operating the system and should need to contact only one vendor to obtain support.

A **service bureau** is a firm providing information processing services, including software and hardware, for a fee. The service bureau owns and manages the software and hardware, which is installed on the service bureau's property. Most of the services a service bureau provides are on a fee-for-service basis, thus minimizing cost to the contracting organization.

A batch-oriented service bureau converts client source data to machine-readable form, processes the data, and provides the organization with various outputs. In this case, the computer software is usually developed and owned by the service bureau. The outsourcing of data entry functions to service bureaus located at international locations, such as Singapore or India, is a recent application of this batch-oriented service bureau concept.

A time-sharing service bureau is accessed via PCs or other devices located in the contracting organization. Transactions and other data are keyed into these devices, and some outputs are returned directly to the organization via these devices. Large printed outputs are spooled at the service bureau. Some software organizations use through a time-sharing service bureau is developed by the organization with the service bureau developing the remainder.

Systems integrators are consulting/systems development firms that develop and install systems under contract. Some of the major players in the systems integration market are Deloitte Consulting, Cap Gemini, BearingPoint, Accenture, and IBM Consulting. Advantages to using systems integrators and consultants to develop systems include:

- The project involves a substantial upgrade in technology that is beyond available in-house expertise. Consulting firms have broad experience and knowledge of specialty and leading-edge technology.

- The organization is not accustomed to change and to projects of this type. Consulting firms have this experience and may specialize in organization change.

- Quick action must be taken to catch up with aggressive competition. Consultant expertise is flexible in that it should be readily available and can be acquired for only the required service.

CONTROLS There is evidence, however, that the use of systems integrators does not always work. For example, one study looked at 16,000 IT projects and found that none of the projects that had heavy participation by big systems integrators were completed on time and within budget![1] Technology Excerpt S1.1 proposes seven steps to preventing these disasters.

ENTERPRISE SYSTEMS

E-BUSINESS

In general, **outsourcing** (often called **co-sourcing**) is the assignment of an internal function to an outside vendor. An organization can outsource its accounting, legal, data processing, strategic planning, manufacturing functions, and so on. There are some who believe that an organization can outsource nearly *all* its functions, thereby creating a so-called "virtual" organization. Since 1989, when the Eastman Kodak Company signed an agreement with IBM whereby IBM would own and operate Kodak's data centers, *outsourcing* has been a viable option for organizations wishing to have an outsider provide some or all of their information systems services.

A rapidly developing segment of the outsourcing market is the *application service provider (ASP)*. Technology Summary S1.1 describes ASPs and summarizes some ASP services. ASPs are similar to service bureaus and other outsourcing options. The ASP, however, provides its services via an easy-to-use Web browser over public networks, rather than more expensive private lines. Several ASPs exist that specialize in providing ERP services to organizations. As the current generation of ERP systems move to Web-enabled clients that function through the use of browser software, the usability and functionality of ERP systems in an ASP environment are becoming less complex and making this model of delivery even more cost effective.

An organization should consider carefully the type of applications that it outsources. The outsourcing of mission-critical applications and those that provide distinction and strategic advantage should probably be avoided, keeping those applications in-house.

---

[1] Geoffrey James, "IT Fiascoes . . . and How to Avoid Them," *Datamation* (November 1997): 87.

Technology Excerpt S1.1

Guidelines for Effective Use of Systems Integrators

The following seven steps may help prevent the disastrous situations associated with IT projects led by systems integrators (SI).

1. Before submitting a request for proposal, define the key project objectives and measures of success. If these can't be defined, don't proceed.
2. Review the SI proposal to determine that due diligence was used in developing the proposal and that the project sponsors—IT and business process owners—understand the proposed solution.
3. Break the project into chunks of six months and tie contract payments to specific milestones.
4. Ensure that the roles and responsibilities of the SI and sponsoring team members have been defined and that the qualifications of these team members have been determined.
5. At project kickoff determine high-risk factors and contingency plans to deal with those factors.
6. The project sponsor must meet regularly with the project manager to determine that the project is progressing as planned.
7. Before completing the project, ensure the achievement of project objectives and milestones.

Source: Excerpted from Gopal K. Kapur, "Happier Projects," *Computerworld* (May 29, 2000): 48.

Technology Summary S1.1

Application Service Provider (ASP)

An **application service provider (ASP)** offers an outsourcing mechanism whereby it hosts, manages, and provides access to application software and hardware over the Internet to multiple customers. The fee is really a rental based on usage, similar to the rental pricing model used by service bureaus. Some ASPs provide service for free, obtaining revenue from advertising and the sale of other services. ASPs, like most external sources of software (and hardware), such as the service bureau, relieve the organization of the burden of developing (or even buying) and installing software (and hardware). Since ASPs are accessed over the Internet, a user needs only a Web browser and an inexpensive PC or Internet appliance to obtain the ASP service.

When using an ASP, a user obtains constantly updated software (similar to a service bureau). The user does not need to install or update software on a client *or* a server and does not need to hire the technical staff to operate the application. ASPs are a good choice for non-critical, niche applications, such as human resources and employee travel and expense reporting and disbursement.

They may be too important to hand over to another organization. Support applications—those that are not primary processes in the value chain, such as human resources and accounting—might be better outsourcing candidates.

Acquiring an AIS from External Parties

An organization should consider the financial implications of the decision to develop (make) versus buy. Because software vendors can allocate software development costs across many products and across multiple copies of each product, the prices they charge to recover development costs are usually substantially less than the organization would pay to develop the package in-house. Generally, software developed in-house for a mainframe computer can cost up to 10 times more than purchased software. Additionally, annual maintenance of in-house software is typically 50 percent of the development cost, while annual maintenance for purchased software normally costs only 25 percent of the purchase price.

To increase the potential market for a software package, vendors develop packages for a wide audience. This strategy leads to products that seldom possess characteristics exactly matching any particular organization's requirements. Organizations not satisfied with these generic packages can contract with a vendor to modify one of the vendor's existing software packages or develop a custom-tailored software package written specifically to meet the organization's unique requirements.

ENTERPRISE SYSTEMS

What is the "bottom line"? We believe it is this: When a *suitable* standard package exists, buy it rather than try to reinvent it in-house. Notice the emphasis on *suitable*. Other considerations must include the organization's internal resources (personnel, capital) and available vendor support. In this chapter we will investigate one alternative means of acquiring an accounting system; that is, we will examine the process of procuring an accounting information system from an external vendor. In Chapter S2 of this supplement, we will study the issues involved with developing information systems in-house.

We first introduce you to a structured AIS acquisition process, which is comprised of four distinct phases: analysis, selection, implementation, and operation. This cycle is depicted in Figure S1.1 and summarized in Table S1.1 (page 8). In the AIS analysis phase, we will discuss two key steps: conducting a preliminary survey (bubble 1.0) and performing a needs analysis (bubble 2.0). In the second phase, AIS selection, we will examine another two steps: evaluating feasible AIS solutions (bubble 3.0) and determining the final solution (bubble 4.0). Although the AIS implementation (bubble 5.0) and AIS operation (bubbles 6.0 and 7.0) phases are illustrated in Figure S1.1, we will defer discussion of these latter two phases until Chapter S4 of this supplement, as the issues involved mirror the implementation and operation of a custom-designed AIS (i.e., an AIS developed in-house).

The CD accompanying this supplement includes *The Accounting Library*, a software program that accountants can use to help narrow-down a potential subset of commercially available accounting systems, depending on the organizational need requirements. We will refer to and use this program when discussing the AIS selection phase. *The Accounting Library* is an invaluable tool, not only for classroom learning, but also for practicing accountants. In all likelihood, you will someday be involved with varying aspect(s) of acquiring and implementing a commercially available AIS.

Accountants Involvement in AIS Acquisition

This chapter can be vitally important to your career, for it walks you through a structured approach to acquiring an AIS from an external vendor. Let us examine some of the roles you might eventually play in the AIS acquisition process.

- *User.* Whether you are a staff accountant, controller, or chief financial officer, you will be using an AIS on a regular basis. In any of these roles, you might be a business process owner as well, which means that you will be responsible for (or own) certain data sets (such as payroll, general ledger, or customer billing data). As such, you very well could be the person who initiates the AIS acquisition cycle, since you

Figure S1.1 AIS Acquisition Cycle

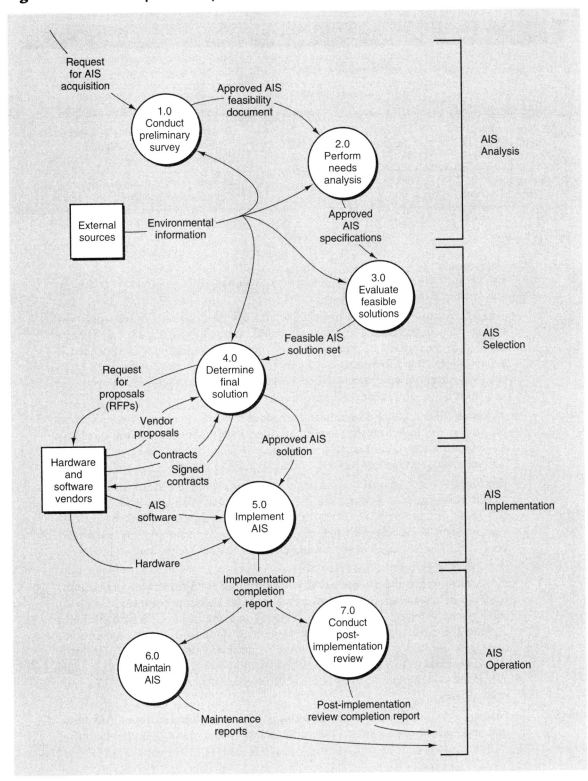

Table S1.1 AIS Acquisition Phases, Purposes, and Tasks*

Phase	Purpose	Tasks
AIS Analysis (bubbles 1.0 and 2.0)	Develop specifications for a new accounting information system.	Study the problem and the environment. Conduct a needs analysis.
AIS Selection (bubbles 3.0 and 4.0)	Purchase an appropriate system.	Evaluate alternative AIS solutions. Choose AIS software and hardware.
AIS Implementation (bubble 5.0)	Successfully switch from the old to the new AIS.	Devise implementation plans, system tests, and training programs. Convert to new system.
AIS Operation (bubbles 6.0 and 7.0)	Use the new system.	Perform systems maintenance. Conduct post-implementation review.

* Refers to Figure S1.1.

will be in prime position to recognize deficiencies and incompatibilities related to the existing AIS.

- *Analyst.* Because you will be intimately familiar with functionality and controllability aspects of accounting systems, you could be asked to participate on a systems analysis team to conduct a preliminary survey used to determine what is needed in a new AIS. Even in those situations where the accountant is not familiar with a particular business process, they can contribute the skills that they have in acquiring and documenting descriptions of processes.

- *Purchaser.* You could also become a member of the AIS selection team. In this capacity, you will have to match the organization's requirements with the capability of various commercially available accounting systems, evaluate a set of potential AIS solutions, and help to make the final purchase selection.

- *Implementer.* Once the AIS is purchased, it is time to switch the old with the new. This is much easier said than done. You could become involved with this delicate and vitally important phase of the acquisition cycle. If so, you will have to be equally adept at dealing with people, accounting, and technology. In particular, your intricate knowledge of accounting and information technology will help you to be successful in this role.

- *Consultant.* While the Sarbanes-Oxley Act prohibits CPA firms who audit a public company to also serve as systems consultants for the same company,[2] AIS consulting is nevertheless alive and well. While all but one major CPA firm (Deloitte Touche Tohmatsu) has spun-off their consulting divisions into separate entities, these new consulting companies continue to need accountants. Also, CPA firms still consult (they often call themselves "business advisors"), just not for their audit clients. As a consultant, you can become involved with any or all of the AIS acquisition phases.

CONTROLS
- *Internal Auditor.* Because internal auditors are knowledgeable about AIS function and control requirements, they often serve as advisors or consultants during

---

[2] The rationale for this change was to prevent auditors from assessing the quality (i.e., auditing) of the work performed by members of their own firm. To do so would violate their independence in appearance or in fact.

the acquisition cycle. Also, as agents of management and the board of directors, internal auditors ensure that the acquisition team has followed the organization's standard procedures for systems acquisition and that the process has been efficient and effective.

- *External Auditor.* As an external auditor, you will conduct an internal control assessment. During your assessment, you will have to determine how changes in the AIS might have affected overall audit risk. As discussed in Chapter 7 of the textbook, professional guidance in this regard is found in Statement on Auditing Standards (SAS) 94, entitled "The Effect of Information Technology on the Auditor's Consideration of Internal Control in a Financial Statement Audit." Thus, external auditors will review the acquisition cycle, and assess if and how internal controls have been impacted.

As just described and summarized in Table S1.2, accountants can play many valuable roles in the AIS acquisition cycle. Will you eventually find yourself in one or more of these roles?—most likely YES! If you are saying to yourself "I don't like this computer stuff, I just want to be an accountant," you might consider changing majors now. The natural marriage of accounting and information technology cannot be escaped, as the lines between the two have been forever blurred. For instance, consider the global thrust toward enterprise systems and e-Business. Accounting is no longer an isolated functional

ENTERPRISE SYSTEMS

E-BUSINESS

Table S1.2 Accountants' Involvement in AIS Acquisition

Accountant Type	How Involved in Development
User	As an employee of the organization, an accountant can become involved in the systems acquisition cycle as the user of the system, the business process owner, or the requester of the system changes. The accountant might well join the acquisition team.
Analyst	As an employee member of the acquisition team who possesses accounting and information technology knowledge, the accountant can be a valuable contributor to the systems survey and needs analysis tasks.
Purchaser	The accountant can play an instrumental role in identifying the subset of commercially available accounting software that meets the organization's needs and selecting the final system for purchase.
Implementer	As an implementer, the accountant could be involved in change management issues and/or the technical aspects of converting data, software, and hardware from the old to the new AIS.
Consultant	Hired from outside the organization—typically a management consulting firm—the accountant can undertake many of the activities in a systems acquisition project.
Internal auditor	Internal and information technology (IT) auditors review systems and make recommendations that lead to system changes. Also, they review acquisition projects to ensure that systems are acquired efficiently and effectively and that the systems being purchased will have sufficient internal controls and will be auditable.
External auditor	An independent external auditor must review the systems that produce financial statements. If the auditor finds inefficient systems, he notifies management in the management letter. If he finds inadequate controls, he notifies management and may alter the audit. Recommendations to management may lead to the initiation of the AIS acquisition cycle.

area within an organization; instead, the AIS is deeply rooted, through technology, into all business processes. This is precisely why you are studying the topic of accounting information systems in your curriculum.

The synopsis at the beginning of this chapter cited an instance where a company called FoxMeyer Drug attempted to implement a commercially available ERP system (SAP), but failed. While there were many complex and interrelated reasons for the failure, had FoxMeyer followed a structured AIS acquisition cycle, it might have averted disaster. While no implementation is fail-proof, your odds of success are considerably improved if you methodically plan and execute the AIS acquisition cycle.

Our discussions of the challenges facing organizations today lead us to the following *AIS acquisition objectives*:

- To acquire an AIS that satisfies an organization's strategic informational and operational needs. Note that this objective relates to the *outcome* (the AIS).

- To acquire an AIS in an efficient and effective manner. Note that this objective relates more to the acquisition *process* than to its outcome.

Achieving AIS Acquisition Objectives

Surprisingly, many organizations fail to achieve their AIS acquisition objectives for a variety of reasons. Although we cannot catalog all the reasons, we can summarize a few here:

- *Lack of senior management support for and involvement in AIS acquisitions.* Analysts and users of information systems watch senior management to determine which information systems acquisition projects are important, and act accordingly by shifting their efforts away from any project not receiving sufficient attention. In addition, management can ensure that adequate resources, as well as budgetary control over use of such resources, are dedicated to the acquisition project.

- *Shifting user needs.* User requirements for accounting systems are constantly changing, causing the need for the new or modified system. When these changes occur *during* an acquisition process, the acquisition team may be faced with the challenge of acquiring an AIS whose objectives keep changing as the project unfolds. The project team must anticipate and manage these shifts and continuously review priorities to ensure that the new system's most critical features are delivered.

- *Emerging technologies.* When an organization tries to create a competitive advantage by applying advanced information technology, it generally finds that attaining systems acquisition objectives is more difficult because personnel are not familiar with the technology making the cost of development, and risk of failure, higher. Also, some acquisition and implementation projects take a great deal of time (between one and two years) and during that period advanced technology could render certain automated business processes obsolete.

- *Lack of standard project management and AIS acquisition methodologies.* Some organizations do not formalize their project management and systems acquisition methodologies, thereby making it difficult to consistently complete acquisitions and related implementations on time or within budget.

ENTERPRISE SYSTEMS

- *Failure to appreciate and act on strategic, organizational, and business process changes that may be required.* The successful implementation of an enterprise system, which embeds the AIS throughout, normally requires that the organization change its structure, business processes, and manner of conducting business to conform to the logic of the enterprise software. Failure to do so leads to systems that operate less than optimally, if at all.

- *Resistance to change.* People have a natural tendency to resist change, and AIS acquisition projects signal changes—often radical—in the workplace. *Business process reengineering* often accompanies AIS acquisitions. If employees perceive that the acquisition project will result in personnel cutbacks, they will dig in their heels, thus dooming the acquisition project to failure from the outset. Personnel cutbacks often result when reengineering projects attempt to "downsize" (or "rightsize"), hence, fear and resentment could thwart the implementation effort.
- *Lack of user participation.* Users must participate in the acquisition effort to define their requirements, feel ownership for project success, and work to resolve acquisition problems. User participation also helps reduce user resistance to change.
- *Inadequate testing and user training.* New accounting systems must be tested before installed to determine if they will operate correctly. Users must be trained to effectively utilize the new system.

To overcome these and other problems, organizations must execute the AIS acquisition process efficiently and effectively. This chapter, along with Chapters S2 and S3 of this supplement, discuss ways to successfully execute systems acquisition and development processes. One approach aimed at reducing the risk of AIS acquisition and systems development failure is to employ sound project management practices.

Project Management

Poor project management often plays a significant role in IT project failures. For instance, the following project management items are commonly associated with failed projects:[3]

- Underestimation of the time to complete the project.
- Inadequate attention by senior management.
- Underestimation of necessary resources.
- Underestimation of project size and scope.
- Inadequate project control mechanisms.
- Changing systems specifications.
- Inadequate planning.

To effectively manage projects, organizations should adopt a management framework that includes the following elements:

- User participation in defining and authorizing the project.
- Assignment of appropriate staff to the project, along with specific definitions of their responsibilities and authorities.
- A clear written statement of the project nature and scope.
- A feasibility study that serves as the basis for senior management approval to proceed with the project.
- A project master plan, including realistic time and cost estimates, to facilitate project control.

---

[3] *Why Do IT Projects Fail? (and how to avoid such failures)*, (Mission Viejo, CA: Hitech Dimensions, Inc., August 2002).

- A risk management program to identify and handle risks associated with each project.
- Division of the project into manageable chunks, often called phases. In turn, phases should be subdivided into steps, and steps into tasks.
- Documentation and approval of work accomplished in one phase before working on the next phase.

Project management—particularly early in the AIS acquisition cycle—ultimately can determine the success of the project. You should note that the recommended project management framework is embedded into the AIS acquisition cycle, as explained next.

AIS ANALYSIS

The AIS analysis phase is comprised of two steps: conducting a preliminary AIS survey and performing an AIS needs analysis. These are critical steps in the AIS acquisition cycle because it is during this early phase when the feasibility of acquiring an AIS is determined and the specific organizational business process needs are matched to the newly acquired AIS. Let's start by examining the preliminary survey.

Conduct Preliminary Survey

A preliminary AIS survey—the first step in the AIS analysis phase—is initiated when the strategic information technology plan prescribes or when a user requests an acquisition. In *planned* reviews, acquisition of an AIS might coincide with anticipated changes in business processes or models; accordingly, the motivation for changing systems would be to facilitate the strategic objectives of the organization. In *requested* reviews, users might be concerned about the existence of one or more problems (e.g., functional or control) with the current AIS, and the organization conducts the preliminary survey to determine the existence, nature, and extent of the problems, as well as the feasibility of acquiring a new system.

The purpose of the systems survey is to investigate AIS problems and to decide on a course of action. One course of action may be to proceed with the acquisition. But, another outcome could be to abandon the proposed acquisition either because the existing AIS already meets the organization's strategic objectives or because it is deemed infeasible to continue. The intermediate tasks associated with the preliminary AIS survey (depicted in Figure S1.2) are gather facts (bubble 1.1), perform feasibility study (bubble 1.2), devise project plan (bubble 1.3), and obtain approvals (bubble 1.4) as discussed next.

Gather Facts
The first intermediate task is to *gather facts* in order to:

- Determine whether a problem exists.
- Refine the nature of the problem.
- Determine the scope of the problem.
- Obtain information to conduct a preliminary feasibility study.
- Devise a plan for conducting the analysis.

The analyst is trying to determine what the AIS does now and what management and users would like it to do in the future. To determine what the AIS is currently doing,

Figure S1.2 **Preliminary Survey Tasks and Documents**

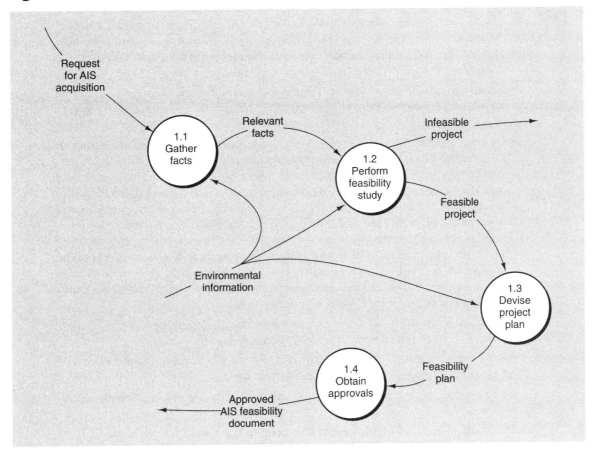

we would review the existing system's documentation and examine the system's operation. The documentation may be inadequate, out-of-date, or both, and the analyst must compare the documentation to actual operations and modify as needed to ensure that the development project proceeds with adequate understanding of the existing situation. To determine what the system should be doing, we will obtain information from users and authoritative sources. For example, we might review a *control matrix* to determine a process' goals, control goals, and recommended control plans. We could also conduct an Internet search to find out the latest functionality of accounting systems.

The extent of fact gathering must be consistent with cost and time constraints imposed on the systems survey. That is, the systems survey must be conducted as *quickly* and as *inexpensively* as possible, yet still accomplish its goals. If the project goes beyond the systems survey, additional, more detailed facts will be gathered during *needs analysis*.

Systems analysts use a number of tools and methods to gather facts, such as interviews with key users, surveys of all affected parties, reviews of documentation maintained within the organization, examination of relevant documentation external to the organization, observations of how the AIS functions within the organizational environment, and database/file reviews related to which data are affected and when during business event processing. Once all salient and relevant facts are gathered, the next intermediate step is the preliminary feasibility study.

Perform Feasibility Study

Having completed the task of gathering and documenting facts, an analyst has a good understanding of what the AIS should do and what it actually does. The analyst undertakes the second systems survey task, the *preliminary feasibility study*, to determine how difficult it will be to close the gap between what the existing system does and what the new system should do. There are three aspects of feasibility:

- **Technical feasibility.** A problem has a technically feasible solution if it can be solved using available (already possessed or obtainable) hardware and software technology.

- **Operational feasibility.** A problem has an operationally feasible solution if it can be solved given the organization's available (already possessed or obtainable) personnel and procedures. In assessing this aspect of feasibility, the analyst should consider behavioral reactions to the systems change. Timing and scheduling may also be factors. An organization may have the available resources but cannot or will not commit them to a particular project at this time because, for instance, union rules might prohibit the automation of certain jobs (see Technology Application S1.1) or resistance to change might be deemed to be so volatile that success of the implementation is in serious jeopardy from the onset. They may wish to scale down a project, take an alternative course of action, or break the project into smaller projects to better fit their scheduling needs.

- **Economic feasibility.** Determining economic feasibility can be a bit more complex. A problem has an economically feasible solution if:

- Net benefit estimates (benefits minus costs) for the AIS acquisition meet or exceed a minimum threshold set by the organization.

- The project compares favorably to competing uses for the organization's resources.

Estimating project costs and benefits this early in the acquisition cycle might seem premature—after all, we know very little about the new system. But management must decide *now* whether to proceed. Therefore, to make that decision, management must know preliminary estimated costs and benefits of the acquisition, no matter how roughly estimated. Typically, costs are easier to determine (most of them are readily quantifiable, such as dollars spent on software, hardware, and personnel) and occur earlier in the system's life cycle. Benefits are more difficult to estimate (many benefits are qualitative, such as improved customer satisfaction and employee loyalty) and occur over a longer period of time.

Analysts use tools, such as capital budgeting models, to determine the economic viability of each acquisition option. Theoretically, the organization should go forward with any project whose *payback* period is less than an acceptable threshold and/or whose positive *net present value* (NPV) or *internal rate of return* (IRR) is at or above a desired benchmark, or whose cost can be *charged back* to users of the new system. In the *long run*, only projects whose return is inadequate should be rejected. In reality, however, *short-run* financing considerations can force an organization to go forward with a limited set of projects that have an acceptable return, because the organization simply cannot afford to pursue all feasible projects.

Devise Project Plan

As discussed earlier, good project management is the key to best ensuring the success of a systems acquisition project. Proper control over a project becomes more important as

Technology Application S1.1

Operational Feasibility Outweighs Technical and Economic Feasibility

A small software development company located in southwest Texas, we'll call it SuperSolutions, has a big idea. The software company specializes in writing various business process applications for newspaper companies. SuperSolutions recognizes that the process of typesetting, building, printing, and billing newspaper advertisements is extremely time-consuming. For instance, say that an automobile dealer wants to place an advertisement in the paper, complete with pictures and descriptions of various cars and trucks, and approve the final copy. First, the art department builds the ad by clipping pictures of appropriate automobiles from a library of art books, enters necessary words and phrases (i.e., ad copy) into a computer, prints the ad copy using a very expensive typesetter, and manually builds the ad, complete with a border and other eye-catching details. Next, the ad is manually placed on a specific newspaper page, often around editorial copy that has already undergone similar typesetting and building processes. Each completed newspaper page is then turned into a negative image (using an expensive camera) that is used to burn the image onto an aluminum plate, which is then used then to transfer the image onto newsprint using a newspaper press. Once the newspaper is distributed, the accounting office has to measure the size of each ad and bill the appropriate rate to the customer.

SuperSolutions developed a suite of interlinked applications where the art work, ad copy, and editorial copy can be entered into a computer, where it is automatically placed and organized onto newspaper pages. The image is then burned directly to the aluminum plate—totally skipping the typesetting and manual page-building processes. Plus, once the paper is distributed, customer billing is automatic. The labor and materials savings are enormous. When attempting to sell the system to a mid-sized newspaper in Oklahoma, the payback period for the entire suite of software and related computer equipment was a mere eight months—mainly because it would trim 108 jobs (10 percent) from the payroll. The president of the potential client was fascinated and immediately ordered the complete package. He claimed that the stockholders would be thrilled with the improved bottom-line performance of the company. A few weeks later, the president called SuperSolutions and abruptly cancelled the order. Why? The typesetting labor union refused to allow termination of the affected jobs. This is a vivid example of how a project can pass economic and technical feasibility tests, but fail on operational feasibility. Interestingly, this brings up sensitive social and ethical issues surrounding the integration of computer technology into organizations when the resulting impact is lost jobs. How do you feel about this?

the risks of failure increase. Some of these risks, many of which are discovered during the feasibility study, include:[4]

- *Project size* (both absolute and compared to other IT projects). Size is measured by staffing, costs, time, and number of organizational units affected.
- *Degree of definition*. Projects that are well defined in terms of their outputs and the steps necessary to obtain those outputs are less risky than those that require user and developer judgment.

---

[4] Nancy Bagranoff, Stephanie Bryant, and James Hunton, *Core Concepts of Consulting for Accountants* (New York: Wiley Press, 2002).

- *Experience with technology.* Risk increases as the organization's experience with the relevant technology decreases.

- *Organizational readiness.* This aspect of operational feasibility addresses the organization's experience with management of similar projects, as well as management and user preparation for and commitment to this project.

Although project management cannot address all risks, it is an important element in minimizing their impact, thus optimizing the odds of success.

If the preliminary AIS feasibility evaluation indicates that further analysis of the problem is warranted, the analyst devises a **project plan**, which is a statement of a project's scope, timetable, resources required to complete the project, and the project's costs. The project plan includes a *broad* plan for the *entire* development, as well as a *specific* plan for *needs analysis*—the next acquisition step. The project plan typically includes:

- Estimated project scope.
- Recommended acquisition team structure, members, and leaders.
- Required tasks.
- Required personnel skills.
- Sources of required information.
- Estimated analysis costs.
- Timetable and estimated costs for the entire acquisition and implementation.

Project plans are developed in order to:

- *Provide a means to schedule the use of required resources.* What personnel and funds will be required and when?

- *Indicate major project milestones to monitor the project's progress.* Is the project on schedule? Has the project provided the required deliverables?

- *Forecast the project budget, which is used to authorize project continuation.* Given the project's progress to date, should additional funds be expended for this step? For the next step?

- *Furnish guidelines for making a go or no-go decision.* Are the costs and benefits as projected? Is the utilization of these resources (monetary and personnel) in the best interest of the organization at this time?

- *Offer a framework by which management can determine the reasonableness and completeness of the project's steps.* Is there a complete list of tasks, and are these tasks properly matched with the required skills? Are the proper information sources being investigated?

Obtain Approvals

The feasibility plan output from bubble 1.3 in Figure S1.2 (page 13) represents a *draft* of the final report. Prior to completing the preliminary AIS survey, the analyst must *obtain approvals (signoffs)*, which are used to signify approval of both the acquisition process *and* the general description of the system being purchased. Obtaining preliminary survey approvals ensures that the feasibility plan's contents are complete, reasonable, and satisfactory to the major participants. Obtaining agreement on the plan's contents is a key element in the acquisition process because such agreement paves the way for cooperation as the project progresses. These approvals fall into two categories: approvals from users/participants and *management control point* approvals.

User/participant approvals verify the accuracy of any *interviews* or *observations* and the accuracy, completeness, and reasonableness of the survey documentation and conclusions. Any other users indirectly affected by the development effort should sign the feasibility plan to signify knowledge and understanding of the impending needs analysis. For instance, *internal audit* may sign off to signify that development procedures are being followed and that controls are being given proper consideration. The controller might sign off to indicate concurrence with the economic feasibility.

The second type of signoff, called a **management control point**, occurs at a place in the systems acquisition process requiring management approval of further development work (i.e., a go/no-go decision). Upper management control points occur at the end of each step of each acquisition *phase* (e.g., AIS preliminary survey, AIS needs analysis, etc.), whereas project management control points occur at the completion of tasks within each step (e.g., gather facts, perform feasibility study, etc.). *End-of-phase* signoffs by upper management are necessary to ensure that the analyst (or analysis team) follows prescribed procedures and to verify the reasonableness of any assumptions made about such factors as constraints, objectives, and operational feasibility.

As a final step in the AIS analysis phase, the analyst must make requested corrections to the AIS feasibility document, as it summarizes the preliminary survey and serves as the *deliverable* for the step (AIS needs analysis). Between the draft and final versions, corrections can be made for any misunderstandings, misinterpretations, or mistakes. This may involve several iterations between bubbles 1.3 and 1.4 of Figure S1.2 (page 13) until final approval is obtained. The typical contents of an approved feasibility document are summarized in Exhibit S1.1 (page 18).

Perform Needs Analysis

The next step of the AIS analysis phase—perform needs analysis—involves the four tasks depicted in Figure S1.3 (page 19). The tasks are study the current AIS (bubble 2.1), define future AIS needs (bubble 2.2), develop the desired AIS configuration (bubble 2.3), and approve the needs analysis (bubble 2.4).

Study Current AIS

The first task in performing a needs analysis is to understand the current system. This requires evaluations of *physical requirements* and *logical specifications*. Physical requirements include issues such as workload volume, peak processing loads, response times, report layouts, input documents and screens, operating systems, computer hardware, and communication systems. In other words, physical requirements reflect the observable features of the AIS.

Logical specifications describe the internal "reasoning" of the current system, such as how input, processing, and output data are linked; relationships among entities, data attributes, and data tables; and workflow automation processes. That is, logical specifications describe how the accounting information is related within the AIS and across other interconnected systems, such as production, shipping, *customer relationship management*, and so on. With enterprise systems, you will need to consider intricate logical relationships of accounting and other business processes. Further, if the company is engaged in e-Business relationships, logical specifications will most likely extend to externally linked information systems as well.

ENTERPRISE SYSTEMS

E-BUSINESS

Exhibit S1.1 Typical Contents of an Approved Feasibility Document

1. **Executive Summary**
   a. Introduction
   b. Summary of findings
   c. Recommendations

2. **Description of the Problem:** Summary of interviews, observations, and documentation gathered during the survey

3. **Solution Objectives:** Statement of the objectives that a new AIS is to achieve

4. **Constraints:** Statement of restrictions placed on the development, for example, retention of certain computer hardware or procedures in a new system

5. **Preliminary Feasibility Study:** Statement of the economic, technical, and operational feasibility of the proposed system

6. **Development Plans**
   a. Scope of the development
   b. Tasks to be accomplished
   c. Timetable for accomplishing the tasks
   d. Systems development team

7. **Potential Solutions:** Description of a new system's major characteristics

8. **Recommendations:** The analyst's recommendations (proceed or do not proceed, how to proceed)

9. **Approvals**

10. **Attachments**
    a. Request for AIS acquisition
    b. Memoranda
    c. Summaries of observations
    d. Documentation
       (1) Organization charts
       (2) Flowcharts
       (3) Data flow diagrams
       (4) Procedures manuals
    e. Feasibility documentation (e.g., economic feasibility tables)
    f. Planning documents
       (1) Project work plans
       (2) Gantt charts
       (3) PERT charts
       (4) Other schedules

Studying and Documenting Current Logical Specifications. Logical specifications can be documented in various ways. One technique is to illustrate the relationships among entities, processes, data, and data stores using data flow diagrams. For example, assume that the current logical customer sales process for a retail store known as Wally's Retail Bonanza works as shown on Figure S1.4 (page 20).

Basically, a customer requests one or more items from a salesperson, who approves the request (bubble 1.0); the customer pays a cashier for the items (bubble 2.0); the customer receives the items from the warehouse (bubble 3.0); and an inventory specialist posts the inventory release to the master inventory data store (bubble 4.0). Data flow diagrams such as this one are easy for the analyst to draw and others to comprehend. In an analogous manner, logical specifications of all existing business processes under consideration for change need to be documented.

Studying and Documenting Current Physical Requirements. *Please refer to Appendix S1 (page 30) and load* The Accounting Library *on your computer, using the CD provided with this supplement.*

The Accounting Library (TAL)[5] is a needs analysis program that helps in the evaluation of physical requirements and selection of commercially available accounting products (or AIS solutions). The program allows users to indicate and prioritize around

---

[5] *The Accounting Library* is a database published by Charles C. Chewning, Jr., of Solutions. For more information, please go to http://www.accountinglibrary.com.

Figure S1.3 Needs Analysis Tasks and Documents

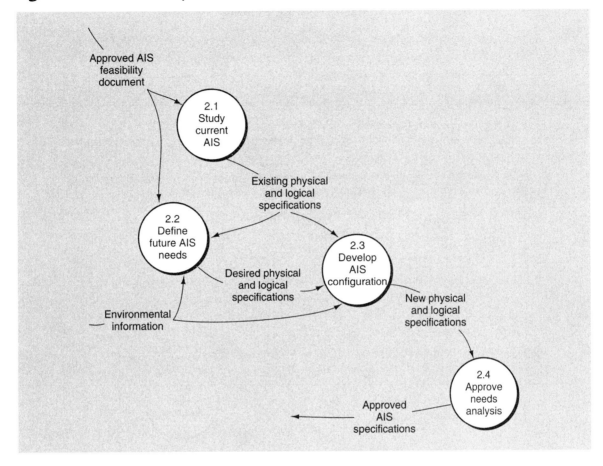

4,000 *need requirements.* Based on the users' defined needs, TAL selects a set of potential AIS solutions, from which companies can choose the one they would like to purchase. We will learn more about how to use TAL later in this chapter, but for now let's look at some of the specific needs that are included in TAL, as this will help you in framing the types of physical requirements to look for in the current AIS and expect in the future AIS.

Once you have completed the steps outlined in Appendix S1, you should see a screen like the one shown in Figure S1.5 (page 21). In the left-hand frame of the screen, you will see 13 folders, starting with General Ledger and ending with Numerical Requirements. Now, click on the General Ledger folder and you will see five more folders, starting with Chart of Accounts and ending with Financial Statements. Next, click on the Financial Statements folder and you should see a screen like the one shown in Figure S1.6 (page 22).

The first item (or need requirement), which appears in the top right-hand frame of the screen is entitled Print Financial Statements to Screen. This item specifies how important it is for users to be able to view financial statements on the screen (notice the context-sensitive explanations of each need requirement in the bottom, right-hand frame of the screen). The user can leave the Answer field blank if this item is not needed

Figure S1.4 Wally's Retail Bonanza's *Current* Logical
       Specification of Its Sales Ordering Process

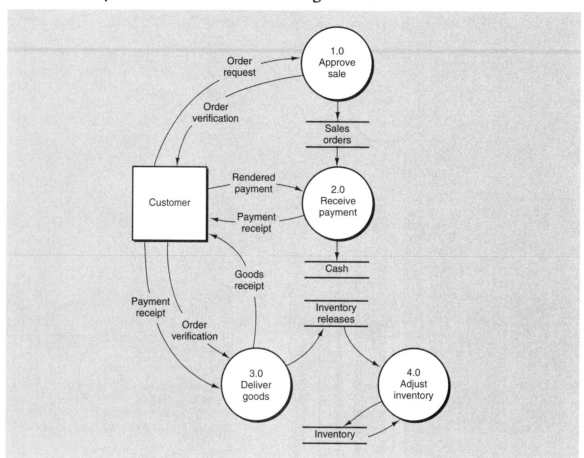

or enter a numeric value from 0 to 9, where a 0 indicates a very low priority of importance and a 9 indicates a very high priority. Scroll down to the bottom of the top, right-hand screen and notice how many requirements are considered in just the Financial Statements section alone. The last category of requirements is General Ledger Month End Schedules. One of its subcategories is Amortization. If you entered, say, a 9 in the Answer field for this item, each AIS solution selected must have this feature. You will find a user's manual and other helpful materials on the CD to which you can refer to learn about all need requirements contained in TAL.

A good way to study physical requirements of a current system is to print an itemized needs definition report from TAL (Reports, Needs Assessment, Itemized Needs Definition. Title the report Test 1). Notice that over 200 pages are printed (to the screen) containing nearly 4,000 need definitions. If, for example, you are considering replacing the current Accounts Payable (AP) portion of the AIS, you could use the needs definitions from the AP section of this report as a guide to determine the current AP capabilities. In the checkbox provided on the report, you can indicate if the current system is capable of addressing each item listed. This helps to document your study of current physical specifications. The next task in performing a needs analysis is to define the future AIS needs.

Figure S1.5 *The Accounting Library* **Requirements Definition Screen**

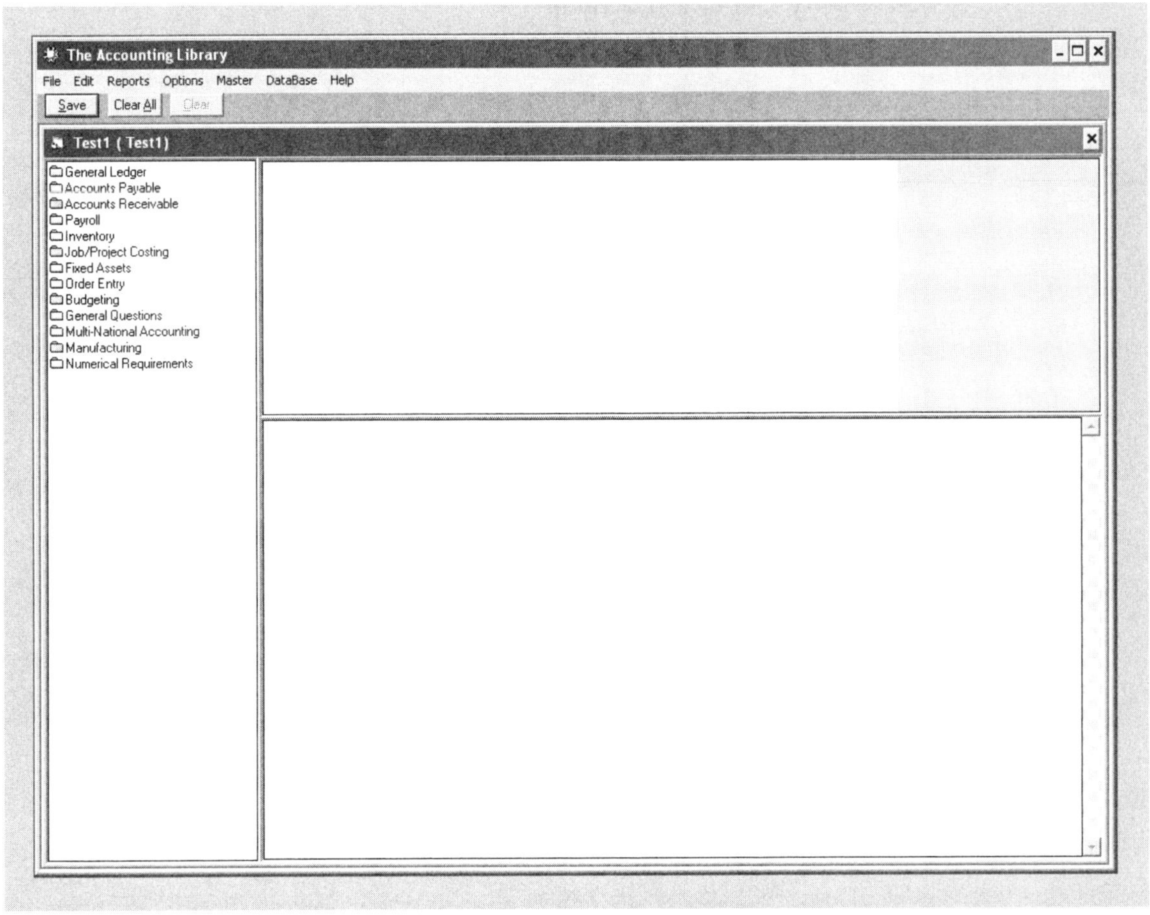

Source: Reprinted with permission of The Accounting Library.

Define Future AIS Needs

Now that we know how the current AIS operates, we must describe how we would like the new system to perform. Once again, you must deal with logical and physical aspects of the new system. Regarding the logical specifications, the analyst or analysis team would have to survey and interview all affected parties before casting the future logical design into concrete. In some cases, this might call for a few tweaks around the edges, or it may involve radical business process reengineering. To illustrate how current and future logical specifications might differ, compare Figure S1.4 to Figure S1.7 (page 23).

Continuing with our Wally's Retail Bonanza example and referring to Figure S1.7, assume that the company wants to change its sales ordering process so that the customer can order items from computer kiosks conveniently located throughout the store. These kiosks automatically check the master inventory table for goods availability, thus eliminating any need for salesperson interaction at this point in the process. Customers can also use this customer self-service feature to look up the latest sales, features, offerings, and so on (bubble 1.0). Once the customer places an order and is ready to pay, he goes to a cashier, who already has access to the sales order information (bubble 2.0). The customer then proceeds to a warehouse representative, who, having access to the sales order

Figure S1.6 *The Accounting Library* **Financial Statements Requirements Definition Screen**

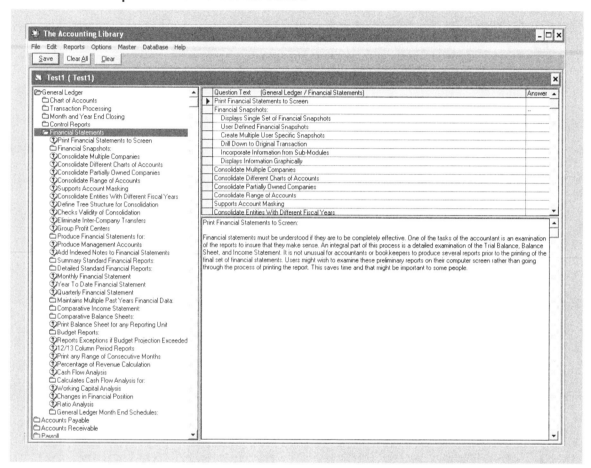

Source: Reprinted with permission of The Accounting Library.

and cash payment information, posts the inventory release simultaneously to the inventory releases (the sales events data) and master inventory table. This is the new logical specification and the selected AIS must meet these needs.

Regarding new physical requirements, you could go to TAL and print out all of the Itemized Need Definition requirements for the Order Entry applications. Checkboxes indicate which needs are applicable. These needs are prioritized from 0 (very low priority) to 9 (very high priority) (see Figure S1.8 on page 24 for a sample report). Explanations for each itemized need can be found either in the manual (on the CD) or by using the context-sensitive explanations of each need requirement in the bottom, right-hand frame of the main TAL screen (see Figure S1.6,). The completed itemized needs analysis will serve to document the future physical requirements.

Develop AIS Configuration

At this point, the analyst or analysis team has documented the existing (as is) and desired (should be) physical requirements and logical specifications. The next task is to develop the final AIS configuration (see Figure S1.3, bubble 2.3, page 19). The best

Figure S1.7 Wally's Retail Bonanza's *Future* Logical
           Specification of Its Sales Ordering Process

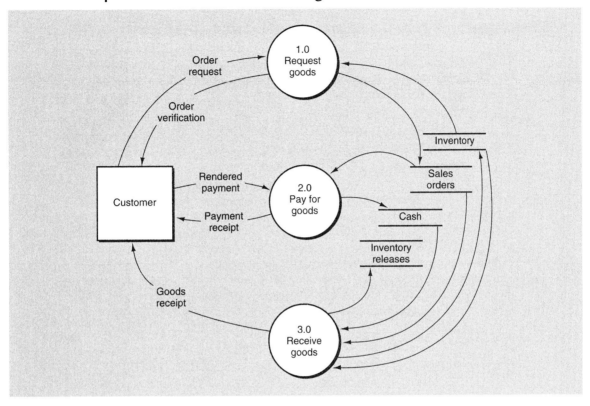

way to complete this task is to conduct a gap analysis, which is an exercise designed to reconcile any differences between the as is and should be requirements.

Recall in the example of Wally's Retail Bonanza, one of the gaps between the existing and new system is that the current system relies on a salesperson to enter sales orders, where in the new system the customer enters her own sales orders via customer self-service kiosks. When scrutinizing this situation, the analysis team realizes that allowing customers not only to order from the kiosks (which is a must-have feature), but also to interrogate the database for sales, colors, sizes, and so on (which is a nice-to-have feature), which increases the number of users and queries and places undue stress on the database. Further, the strategic plan for this project does not include a major upgrade to the database software. In this instance, the analysis team, in consultation with all affected parties, might decide to drop the inquiry feature from the kiosks, at least for now. This example illustrates the type of gap analyses that must be performed. Once all gaps have been reconciled and agreed to, the new physical and logical specifications must be approved.

Approve Needs Analysis
The final task in performing a needs analysis is to obtain needed approvals (see Figure S1.3, bubble 2.4, page 19). Managers who are involved in the AIS acquisition project and key users need to analyze the new physical and logical specifications and approve the needs analysis. This is a very important control feature of the acquisition project, because a go decision here triggers the next phase (AIS selection).

CONTROLS

Figure S1.8 *The Accounting Library* Sample Itemized
Need Definition for the Order Entry System

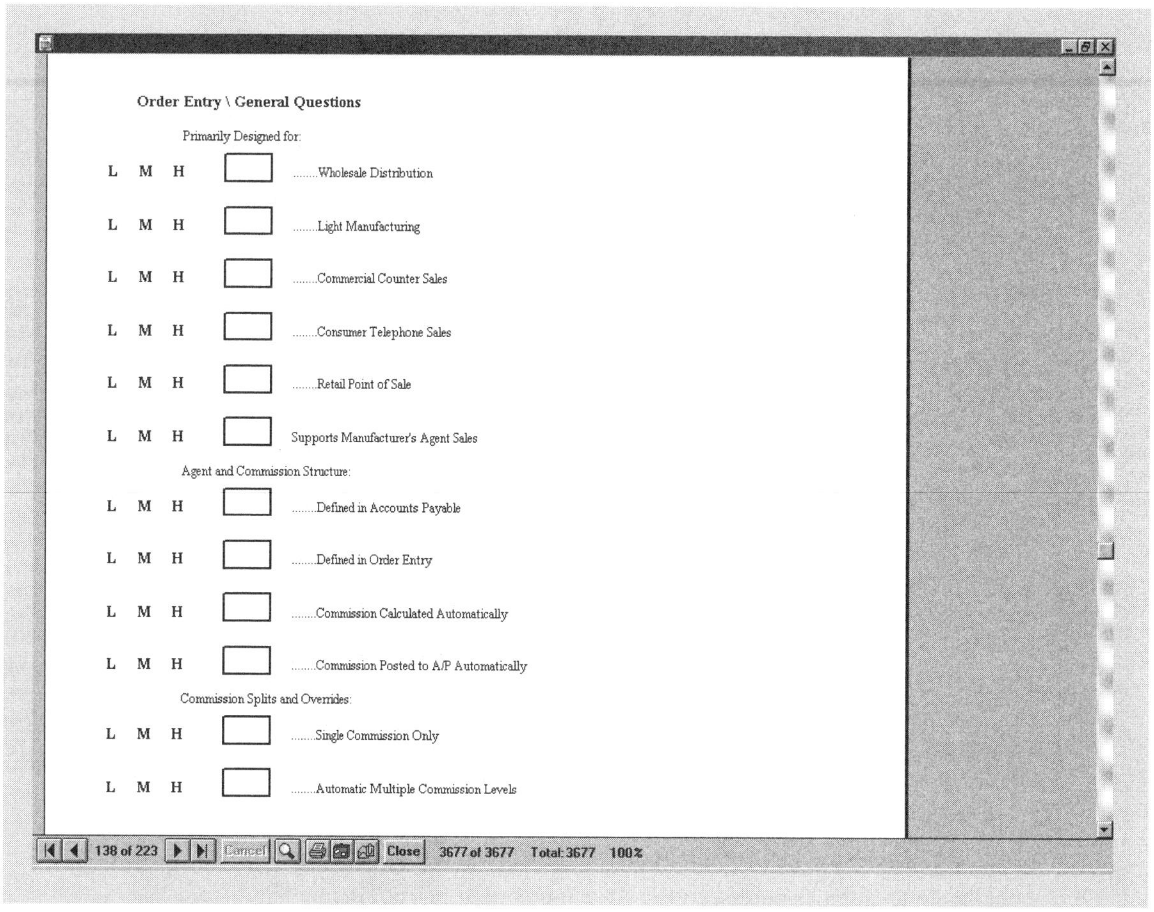

Order Entry \ General Questions

Primarily Designed for:

L	M	H	[ ]	........Wholesale Distribution
L	M	H	[ ]	.......Light Manufacturing
L	M	H	[ ]	.......Commercial Counter Sales
L	M	H	[ ]	.......Consumer Telephone Sales
L	M	H	[ ]	.......Retail Point of Sale
L	M	H	[ ]	Supports Manufacturer's Agent Sales

Agent and Commission Structure:

L	M	H	[ ]	.......Defined in Accounts Payable
L	M	H	[ ]	.......Defined in Order Entry
L	M	H	[ ]	.......Commission Calculated Automatically
L	M	H	[ ]	.......Commission Posted to A/P Automatically

Commission Splits and Overrides:

L	M	H	[ ]	.......Single Commission Only
L	M	H	[ ]	.......Automatic Multiple Commission Levels

138 of 223   Cancel   Close   3677 of 3677   Total: 3677   100%

Source: Reprinted with permission of The Accounting Library.

AIS Selection

As indicated in Figure S1.1 (page 7), selecting the AIS involves two steps—evaluating feasible solutions (bubble 3.0) and determining the final solution (bubble 4.0). Both of these steps and their tasks are discussed next.

Evaluate Feasible Solutions

Evaluating feasible solutions involves two primary tasks (see Figure S1.9)—matching specifications with potential AIS solutions (bubble 3.1) and determining a set of feasible solutions (bubble 3.2).

Match Specifications with Potential Solutions

To match specifications, we will use *The Accounting Library* (TAL). Open the program, click File, Open, and Test 1. Click Clear All to clear all requirements. In the left-hand frame, click the Order Entry folder and then the General Questions folder. Notice in the

Figure S1.9 Feasible Solutions Tasks and Documents

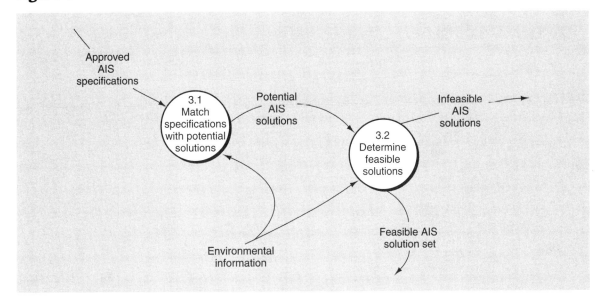

upper right-hand frame, there is an itemized list of need requirements. Let's fill in just a few to give you a feel for how TAL works.

For the following list of needs, enter the numeric values shown (notice for a priority of 9 the system will ask you to verify, because a 9 signifies a critical need, and all AIS solutions that cannot support this need will be automatically eliminated from the feasible set of solutions):

1. Retail point of sale (9)
2. Commissions calculated automatically (9)
3. Supports cash drawer (5)
4. Commission calculations (9)
5. Supports all inventory functions (9)
6. Displays seller's warrantee information (7)
7. Supports restocking (9)

Select Reports, Rank Products, Ranking (the system will ask if you want to save Test 1— answer *yes*). Enter Test 1 for the report name. The software now sorts through all of the accounting system solutions in its database (it may take a little time, depending on the power of your computer). It is matching all requirements with a 9 and trying to match need requirements with priorities less than 9. A report is produced like that shown in Figure S1.10 (page 26).

Notice that ACCPAC, On the Money!, and Mastermind Formula all meet the indicated need requirements. The 100 percent ranking means that all of the 9 requirements are met and the other two requirements that were less than 9 are met at or above the desired priority level. The other solutions that were not eliminated meet the 9 requirements, but do not meet or exceed one or more of the less than 9 requirements.

In a similar fashion, all of the itemized needs would be input into TAL, based on the approved AIS specifications. You should end up with one or more commercially available

Figure S1.10 Sample Product Ranking Report from *The Accounting Library*

The Accounting Library
Test 1
Product Ranking
15 December 2003

Score		Product Name	Version	Vendor Name
57	100%	ACCPAC Advantage Series Enterprise Edition	5.0	ACCPAC International
57	100%	ACCPAC Advantage Series Corporate Edition	5.0	ACCPAC International
57	100%	ACCPAC Advantage Series Small Business Edition	5.0	ACCPAC International
57	100%	ACCPAC Advantage Series Discovery Edition	5.0	ACCPAC International
57	100%	On The Money!	3.1	Parker Systems, Inc.
57	100%	Mastermind Formula	8.0 Build 26	MyBusinessApp
55	96%	One World XE	Jan 2001	J.D. Edwards, Inc.
54	94%	**MAS 500, ©**	6.2	Best Software, Inc.
52	91%	MAX / Great Plains Dynamics	5.5	Keywill ERP, Inc.
52	91%	Alliance Mfg. / Dynamics	5.5	Alliance Manufacturing
50	88%	Advanced Accounting	5.1	Addsum Business Software
50	88%	Flagship World Class Managerial Accounting	5.09	Flagship Systems, Inc.
50	88%	Perfect Software Windows Accounting Series	8.0	Perfect Software
50	88%	Perfect Software LAS/400 Accounting Series	8.0	Perfect Software
48	84%	PeopleSoft	8.0	PeopleSoft, Inc.
48	84%	**Pacifica Professional Accounting for Windows , ©**	8.0	Pacifica Research
47	82%	MISYS / ACCPAC for Windows Corporate Series	4.1	Manufacturing Information Systems
46	81%	SAP R/3	Jan 2001	SAP
46	80%	Fourth Shift 7	7.0	Fourth Shift Corp.
45	79%	Visual AccountMate/SQL	5.1	AccountMate Software Corp.
40	71%	Ramco e Applications	3.1	Ramco Systems Corp.
39	68%	BizTone Financials Enterprise Edition	Build 139	BizTone.com
39	68%	BizTone Financials eXpress Edition	Build 139	BizTone.com
37	65%	Datamodes TM/4 Solutions	TM/4	Datamodes, Inc.
26	45%	Millennium+ Accounting for Microsoft BackOffice	2K	eTek International, Inc.
17	30%	AGRESSO Software	5	Agresso Corp., Inc.
Eliminated		APPGEN Business Software	4.1	Appgen Business Software, Inc.
Eliminated		Axcent	3.0	Axcess Software, Inc.
Eliminated		Down To Earth Business Software	3.4	Synergex International Corp.
Eliminated		GIANT Office Software	4.1	Giant Systems
Eliminated		Myte Myke Software	6.0	M & D Systems, Inc.
Eliminated		Vigilant - Job Costing Accounting	8.2	Vigilant Business Software, Inc.
Eliminated		Vigilant - Manufacturing Accounting	8.2	Vigilant Business Software, Inc.
Eliminated		Vigilant - Point Of Sales Accounting	8.2	Vigilant Business Software, Inc.

1 of 3   Cancel   Close   154 of 154   Total: 154   100%

Source: Reprinted with permission of The Accounting Library.

solutions. If all solutions are eliminated, then perhaps some of the 9 requirements need to be reevaluated, and/or some of the priorities of other requirements need to be lowered. Naturally, this would require the consent of all affected parties. If such compromises cannot be made, then you will have to consider modifying a commercially available solution to fit your business processes and/or developing your own information system (a topic that is considered in Chapters S2 and S3 of this supplement).

Determine Feasible Solutions

In the last step, the universe of available AIS solutions is narrowed down to a set of potential solutions, based on need requirements. But there may be some reasons why one or more solutions in the set cannot be included. For instance, perhaps your company has heard or read poor reviews of one of the vendors. Or maybe you already know that installing one of the solutions will conflict with, or be incompatible with, your operating system and other software applications. There may be other reasons to exclude certain potential AIS solutions at this point. Once the potential set has been reduced, you will end up with a feasible AIS solution set.

Determine Final Solution

The next step in the AIS selection phase is to determine the final solution (see Figure S1.1, bubble 4.0, page 7). This step is comprised of three major tasks (see Figure S1.11)—appraise vendor proposals (bubble 4.1), recommend final solution (bubble 4.2), and approve final solution (bubble 4.3).

Figure S1.11 Final Solution Tasks and Documents

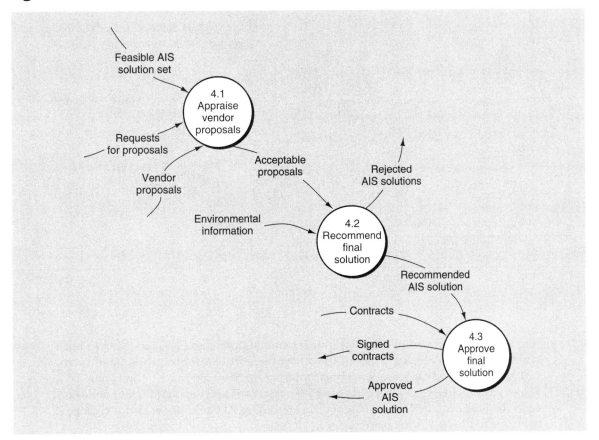

Appraise Vendor Solutions

The first activity in this task is to send requests for proposals (RFP) to prospective vendors who have been identified in the feasible AIS solution set. A RFP is not a legal document; rather, it is a source document asking the vendor if its AIS solution can meet the requestor's need requirements and what the cost would be to purchase the solution. RFP's can be fairly simple and straightforward, or they can be extremely lengthy and complex, depending on factors such as the requesting firm's size, complexity of the proposed system, and so on. At a minimum, the RFP should cover the basic areas shown in Exhibit S1.2 (page 28).

We will not spend any time discussing hardware considerations here, as this topic is very complex. Suffice it to say, though, that one or more members of the AIS acquisition project must be technology-savvy, for the purchased AIS solution must be compatible

Exhibit S1.2 Typical Contents of a Request for Proposal

1. A description of the scope of the request, including a brief description of the hardware, software, and services for which a proposal is requested

2. A description of the AIS including, if applicable, the *logical specification* and *physical requirements*, which in turn include specifications for the:
   - Inputs
   - Outputs
   - Data storage
   - Processes
   - Controls

3. Procedures for submitting proposals, including a timetable for proposal submission, evaluation of proposals, and final decision date

4. Price and budget constraints

5. Vendor information required, including:
   - Contract terms
   - Warranty
   - General company information

6. Hardware performance objectives, such as:
   - Data storage capacities and access requirements
   - Input/output speeds and volumes
   - Data communication requirements
   - Computational demands

7. Software performance objectives, such as:
   - Inputs
   - Required outputs
   - Data table sizes and access requirements
   - Operating system requirements
   - Utilities
   - Language compilers

8. Projected growth requirements, including expected changes in input/output volumes

9. Criteria to be used in evaluating vendor proposals, such as:
   - Ability to meet performance objectives
   - Benchmarks
   - Reliability
   - Documentation
   - Training
   - Backup
   - Maintenance assistance

with existing or proposed information and communications technologies. In all likelihood, technical representatives from the information systems function will be involved with the project and can serve as advisors in this regard. It is important to note, however, that as an accountant, you will need to be conversant with technological terms and concepts, because acquiring, implementing, and operating AIS software is intricately intertwined with the underlying hardware.

Once the RFPs are returned, in the form of vendor proposals, they must be analyzed and compared. Vendors whose AIS solutions meet the RFP requirements, including the requestor's budgetary constraints, are then categorized as acceptable proposals. This solution set (acceptable proposals) now forms the final candidates from which one will be selected.

Recommend Final Solution

You are in the final lap and the pressure is on—it is time to select the winning candidate, as the votes are in and the judges' scores are being tallied. But wait, you should check out your final contender by getting references from companies who are using the vendor's software and searching the Internet for reviews on and comments about the AIS solution. This final decision is very critical, as your organization will have to live a long time with the vendor and product. Choose wisely and carefully. Once the analysis team is satisfied with the final selection, it is time for one last round of approvals.

Approve Final Solution

At a minimum, one or more representatives from upper management, all user groups, and the project manager need to approve the recommended AIS solution. This process might involve an iterative series of questions and answers among all affected parties, but diligently attending to these issues is well worth your time. Once everyone is satisfied, the organization should meet with its legal representative to develop and ratify a contract with the vendor. Logical specifications and physical requirements of the final solution are then forwarded to the implementation team.

AIS IMPLEMENTATION AND OPERATION

As shown on Figure S1.1 (page 7) the next two phases of the AIS acquisition cycle are AIS implementation (bubble 5.0) and operation (bubbles 6.0 and 7.0). As mentioned earlier, implementation and operation issues related to acquired systems are essentially the same as with internally developed systems. Accordingly, we will cover these topics in Chapter S4 of this supplement.

SUMMARY

In this chapter we have introduced to you some of the important issues surrounding the acquisition of a new accounting information systems solution. We described how to conduct the first two phases in the AIS acquisition cycle—AIS analysis and AIS selection. We hope that as you read this chapter you were able to envision how you, as a user, analyst, purchaser, implementer, consultant, or auditor (internal and external) might coordinate or participate in the systems acquisition process. Before we conclude, let us expand on the implications of two key issues.

Accounting information systems are becoming increasingly more complex, from software, hardware, and business integration perspectives. As this trend continues, the mix of accounting and information technology (IT) skills that accountants are expected to possess when they walk in the door is leaning more heavily toward IT than ever before. For example, IT-savvy accountants are now required to ensure that internal controls are integrated into the AIS and that such controls are effectively deployed throughout the organization. Additionally, accountants cannot possibly understand business process integration, workflow automation, and other intra- and interfirm functionalities unless they have a firm grasp on both accounting and IT.

Second, the progressive implementation of enterprise systems, such as *ERP* systems wherein the AIS is embedded throughout, will make project management over acquisitions and related implementations more important and more difficult. These systems affect literally every unit and every person in an organization. If the organization is large and international, as many are, the project management problems are compounded. As a result, most major ERP system vendors provide tools to help manage the implementation process and/or enlist consulting companies that specialize in implementing such systems. Generally, to avoid implementation disasters, most firms outsource all or part of the implementation process to vendors or consultants, as these projects are simply too large and complex for organizations to undertake themselves.

ENTERPRISE SYSTEMS

APPENDIX S1

The Accounting Library (TAL)

1. Insert *The Accounting Library* CD into your CD drive.
2. Select Start then Run on the Windows task bar (bottom, left-hand corner of your screen).
3. Type X: Setup (where X refers to your CD drive letter). Follow the setup instructions.
4. Click on *The Accounting Library* icon (TAL).
5. The first time you initiate TAL, you will be asked to enter your name and the software's serial number. Enter the number located on the CD.
6. Click File and New.
7. Enter Test 1 in both the Question Set Name and Description boxes.
8. A screen like the one depicted in Figure S1.5 (page 21) now appears.
9. Click the Save button to save Test 1 for future use.

REVIEW QUESTIONS

RQ S1-1   What are the alternative ways of purchasing the functionality of commercially available AIS software?

RQ S1-2   What are some reasons for purchasing an AIS solution versus building one in-house?

RQ S1-3   What are the AIS acquisition phases, steps, and tasks?

RQ S1-4   Why and how might accountants become involved in purchasing an AIS?

RQ S1-5   What are the AIS acquisition objectives?

RQ S1-6   How might project management over the AIS acquisition cycle help to improve the odds of success?

RQ S1-7   What might trigger an organization's desire to acquire a new AIS?

RQ S1-8   What is the purpose of a feasibility study?

RQ S1-9   What is a project plan?

RQ S1-10   Where and why are approvals needed during the acquisition cycle?

RQ S1-11   What is the difference between logical specification and physical requirements?

RQ S1-12   How can needs analysis software, such as *The Accounting Library*, help in the AIS acquisition process?

RQ S1-13   What is meant by feasible solutions?

RQ S1-14   What is a request for proposal (RFP)?

RQ S1-15   What elements might be included in an RFP?

RQ S1-16   What should you do before purchasing an AIS solution from a vendor?

DISCUSSION QUESTIONS

DQ S1-1 Discuss several factors affecting (negatively or positively) the achievement of AIS acquisition objectives.

DQ S1-2 The chapter describes two different triggers for the systems acquisition process—a planned, periodic review and user-requested systems development. Compare and contrast those two triggers.

DQ S1-3 How might the absence of an organization's strategic plan for the information system affect the conduct of a preliminary survey? *Hint:* Discuss the potential difficulties of making preliminary survey decisions in the absence of each of the strategic plan components.

DQ S1-4 In doing a preliminary survey for the proposed automation of the cash disbursements system of XYZ Company, the analyst in charge reached the tentative conclusion that Larry Long, the popular cashier with more than 30 years of company service, will be displaced and perhaps asked to consider early retirement. Discuss how this scenario relates to the topic of operational feasibility presented in this chapter. Discuss the potential impact on the success of the new disbursements system.

DQ S1-5 "Choosing among renting, leasing, and purchasing an AIS is strictly a financial decision and should be done by the finance staff." Do you agree? Discuss fully.

DQ S1-6 "There are so many accounting software packages on the market today that no organization should ever have to write its own." Do you agree? Discuss fully.

DQ S1-7 "A vendor would never propose a system that would not meet an organization's needs. Therefore, external validation of vendor proposals is not really needed." Do you agree? Discuss fully.

PROBLEMS

P S1-1 Conduct research of current literature and databases to find reports of systems development project failures. Prepare a report or presentation (as directed by your instructor) describing the failure. Include the elements of feasibility and project risk that may have been miscalculated or mismanaged that led to the project failure.

P S1-2 Conduct research of current literature and databases to find two application service providers (ASPs) who offer accounting information system solutions. Prepare a report or presentation (as directed by your instructor) that compares and contrasts the offerings of each ASP. If you were the CFO of a large, multinational manufacturing company, which ASP would you choose and why?

P S1-3 The CEO of your company has just appointed you as the primary systems analyst on an AIS acquisition project. The CEO has stated that this project has a very high priority for the company. During the preliminary survey, you found that the most important request from management is that the new AIS be capable of handling certain specific budgeting tasks. After interviewing all affected managers and users, you determined that the following budgeting features were essential.

1. Support a roll up budget, where subdivisions' budgets are consolidated into divisions' budgets, which are consolidated into a company-wide budget.
2. Include multiyear budgeting functionality.
3. Allow actual versus budget comparisons for analysis purposes.
4. Maintain a history of all changes made to the budget.
5. Allow for multiple budget revisions in a given fiscal year.
6. Provide for monthly budget reporting.

It is also highly desired, but not critical, that the software be capable of handling capital budgeting projects (priority 8). Other nice-to-have features are support of non-general ledger activities (priority 5) and budget groups (priority 3), and interface capability with a separate internal budgeting module developed by the organization (priority 4). Two low priority items are support for campaign budgets (priority 1) and integration with third-party budgeting systems (priority 0).

Required:

a. Use *The Accounting Library* to develop a list of commercially available software that meets 100 percent of the company's need requirements.

b. Since your company uses a Microsoft operating system and database software, management would like to purchase a Microsoft AIS solution, if possible. Does Microsoft offer an AIS solution? If so, what is the name of the software package?

c. What issues would you consider when narrowing down the set of potential AIS solutions to the set of feasible solutions (assume that management is willing to consider other packages than just Microsoft)?

d. Assuming that you decide on one of the 100 percent ranked solutions indicated by *The Accounting Library*, would the information you now have be sufficient to make a purchase decision? Why? Explain fully.

P S1-4 As treasurer of a large, international manufacturing company, you have been asked to serve as an advisor on your company's AIS acquisition project. Your biggest concern is how the new system will handle multinational accounting. You have told the analysis team that the new system must have the following features.

1. Since your company purchases many materials and supplies from China and Thailand, the system must be able to purchase in foreign currencies.
2. The system must have the ability to send funds electronically using various international banking formats.
3. The accounts receivable invoices must have the capability of being printed in foreign currencies.

4. The system must be able to format the date in Day/Month/Year, since so many of your European affiliates use this format.

5. Euros, value added taxes (VAT), and intrastate taxes in Europe must be handled.

6. Accounts payable checks must have the capability of being printed in foreign currencies.

Other considerations are receiving payments in foreign currencies and single for multiple-currencies (priorities 8). Support for hyperinflationary accounting is a very low priority (0).

Required:

a. Use *The Accounting Library* to develop a list of commercially available software that meets 100 percent of the company's need requirements.

b. What issues would you consider when narrowing down the set of potential AIS solutions to the set of feasible solutions?

c. Assuming that you decide on one of the 100 percent ranked solutions indicated by *The Accounting Library*, would the information you now have be sufficient to make a purchase decision? Why. Explain fully.

d. What if no AIS solution was available based on your stated needs? What might you do next? Explain fully.

KEY TERMS

turnkey system

service bureau

systems integrators

outsourcing (co-sourcing)

application service
provider (ASP)

technical feasibility

operational feasibility

economic feasibility

project plan

management control point

Structured Systems Analysis

Oxford Health Plans, Inc., developed a new computerized information system, called "Pulse," that was to put the company on the IT cutting edge and secure its place in the leadership of its industry. It was not successful. The system was in development for over five years, had 100 outside contractors, and was costing over $20 million per year to develop. When implemented, the system:

- was three to four months behind in getting premium bills to customers.
- left claims unpaid for six or more months. Medical providers were advanced $275 million against these claims.
- could not handle the volume of transactions. For example, new member signup was to take six seconds but took 15 minutes.

As a result, the problems:

- led to customers canceling their memberships, leaving customer rolls inflated by 30,000 and revenues overstated by $111 million.
- resulted in unprocessed claims that led to higher-than-expected losses and refusal of some providers to service Oxford clients.
- generated erroneous data that caused Oxford to write off $94.1 million of uncorrectable accounts receivable leading to a loss in one quarter of $78.2 million ($0.99/share).

How did this happen? Unlike FoxMeyer (see the story at the start of Chapter S1), Oxford had decided to develop their new system in-house but failed at many points along the way from analysis through implementation. Oxford did not have a clear definition of the project and was not prepared to manage it to successful completion. The high turnover of programmers led to a lack of development continuity. The work was poorly done and the new systems inadequately tested. This chapter generally will describe the processes typically employed by systems development teams to avoid the problems encountered by Oxford and to improve the likelihood that their systems development efforts will be successful. Specifically, this chapter will focus on one of the phases of a structured approach to developing information systems—the systems analysis phase.

Learning Objectives

- To know how to develop or modify information systems so that those systems can be directed at achieving an organization's objectives.
- To be able to describe the systems development process and its major phases and steps.
- To understand the nature and importance of the accountant's involvement in systems development.
- To be able to perform relevant portions of the systems analysis phase of developing information systems.
- To be able to describe the goals, tasks, documents, and results of systems analysis.

Synopsis

In Chapter S1 we examined the analysis and selection phases of purchasing an AIS from an external vendor. Sometimes, however, an organization's needs are so unique that a commercial software solution is not available. In such cases, an organization might decide to develop its own information system, accounting or otherwise, using internal skills and resources. This is not for the faint of heart, for developing your own system takes a great deal of time, money, skills, forethought, and leadership. Despite the obstacles, however, it can be the only way to achieve the organization's strategic goals.

In this chapter you will study a structured approach to developing information systems called the systems development life cycle (SDLC). We will examine several ways in which accountants can become involved in the systems development process. Next, we will investigate the first phase of the SDLC, called systems analysis. You will note similarities between the analysis phase of the AIS acquisition cycle covered in Chapter S1 and the SDLC, because many of the same issues arise. The SDLC analysis phase begins with conducting a *systems survey* and performing a *structured systems analysis.*

As a result of decisions made in the systems survey, we know if and how we will proceed with systems development. It is at this point where an organization decides the make (in-house) versus buy choice. If the decision is made to proceed in-house, a structured systems analysis is performed. The procedures in this step must be performed exceptionally well to have any chance of achieving the first of our systems development objectives—to develop systems that meet user needs—because it is during systems analysis that such needs are determined. Without a well-understood and documented target (i.e., user requirements), we cannot hope to have a successful development process.

The needs analysis may appear to be the same, but the stakes are often higher for in-house development. When a system is purchased, the assistance of products such as *The Accounting Library* are employed to select an appropriate solution. The reasonableness of that solution can be tested much earlier in the development process by, for example, assessing a demonstration of the proposed system.

At some point in your professional career you will be on both sides of this process. You will be a system user or business process owner articulating your needs, or you will be a member of the development team that must determine and document such needs. Neither process is easy, but the tools and techniques described in this chapter should help in the documentation of user requirements.

Introduction

The story at the beginning of this chapter cited an instance where a company, Oxford Health Plans, attempted to develop its own information system (IS) but failed to meet the system's and organization's objectives. Unfortunately, the story at Oxford has been repeated many times over across all sizes and types of organizations. On the surface, it seems intuitively appealing to build your own IS that is specifically tailored to the organization's needs. But in reality, this is a difficult undertaking indeed. However, there are circumstances where in-house development is the only reasonable solution. In such cases, organizations should take precautionary measures aimed at reducing the risk of failure to an acceptably low level. For this to happen, the company should follow a structured approach to developing an IS and tightly manage the project at every step of the process.

Systems development comprises the steps undertaken to create, modify, or maintain an organization's information system. These steps, along with the *project management* concepts discussed in Chapter S1, guide the in-house development of information systems. We refer to the **systems development life cycle** (SDLC) as the progression of an information system through the systems development process, from birth through implementation to ongoing use. Systems development is also an important—and sometimes dominant—component of more comprehensive organizational change via *business process reengineering*.

CONTROLLING THE SYSTEMS DEVELOPMENT PROCESS

The *systems development objectives* are as follow:

- To develop an information system that satisfies an organization's informational and operational needs (product-oriented objective).
- To develop an information system in an efficient and effective manner (process-oriented objective).

The key to achieving the first objective is to control the development *process*. Apparently, that is not an easy chore or more organizations would be successful at doing it. We can understand the complexity of the systems development process by comparing it to a construction project. Assume you are in charge of the construction of an industrial park. What problems and questions might you encounter? For instance, you might want to know the following: "How much of the project is whose responsibility?", "Who should handle legal and financial matters?", "Who obtains the building permits?", and "Who is responsible for contacting the tenants/buyers to determine special needs?" The project's size and duration cause another set of problems. How will you coordinate the work of the carpenters, masons, electricians, and plumbers? How will you see that a tenant's special needs are incorporated into the specifications and then into the actual construction?

Information systems developers encounter similar problems. Given such problems, they have concluded that systems development must be carefully controlled and managed by following good project management principles (as discussed in Chapter S1). and the organization's quality assurance framework, including its *systems development life cycle methodology*.

Quality Assurance

The project management framework applies to any project (refer to the framework elements in Chapter S1 on pages 11–12). To ensure that information systems will meet the needs of the customers, projects involving the creation or modification of information systems must also include elements that specifically address the quality of the system being developed.

Quality assurance (QA) addresses the prevention and detection of errors, especially defects in software that may occur during the system development process. By focusing on the procedures employed during the systems development process, QA activities are directed at preventing errors that may occur. QA activities are also directed at testing developed systems to eliminate defects—to ensure that they meet the users' requirements—before systems are implemented. Two of the more prominent sources of guidance for QA are ISO 9000-3 and the Capability Maturity Model (CMM) developed by the Software Engineering Institute (SEI) at Carnegie Mellon University. As you read the following discussion about ISO and CMM, notice that they are process oriented, as QA reflects a process for *controlling* the systems development activities to help achieve development objectives.

ISO 9000-3 is documentation of standards for the processes used to develop, install, and maintain computer software. Developed by the International Organization for Standardization (ISO), these standards state the requirements for what an organization must do to manage the processes that it uses to develop software. The assumption, as with all ISO standards, is that if the ISO 9000-3 standards are followed, the development process will produce a quality software product. ISO defines a quality product as one that conforms to customer requirements. Notice that the ISO concepts of quality products and processes parallel our two systems development objectives. Exhibit S2.1 contains examples of the ISO 9000-3 standards.

Exhibit S2.1 Sample Elements from ISO 9000-3 Guidelines

- Develop quality plans to control all software development projects.
- Make sure that you and your software customer agree on how, products will be accepted, the customer will participate, users will be trained, and changes in requirements will be handled.
- Prepare a software development plan that includes project definition, objectives, schedule, inputs, outputs, risks, assumptions, and control strategies.
- Verify software design outputs by performing design reviews, demonstration, and tests.
- Develop procedures to control software replication, release, and installation.
- Perform software validation and acceptance tests.
- Develop procedures to control your software maintenance.

Source: Adapted from Praxion Research Group Limited, "ISO 9000-3 1997 Guidelines in Plain English: Guidelines for Applying ISO 9001 1994 to Computer Software," http://praxiom.com/iso-9000-3.htm, November 30, 2001.

The **Capability Maturity Model® (SW-CMM®) for Software** is a model that helps organizations evaluate the effectiveness of their software development processes and identify the key practices required to increase the maturity of those processes. Exhibit S2.2 (page 38) describes the five SW-CMM maturity levels, and the key principles and practices for each. Notice, for example, that project management is a key indicator that an organization has attained level 2. The Software Engineering Institute believes that predictability, effectiveness, and control of an organization's software processes improve as the organization moves up the five levels. However, moving from level 1 to level 2 may take an organization two years or more. Moving from level 2 to 3 may take another two years.

Systems Development Methodology

The portion of an organization's quality assurance framework that addresses the development of entire information systems (not just the software) is called the systems development methodology. A **systems development methodology** (also known as **systems development life cycle (SDLC) methodology**) is a formalized, standardized, documented set of activities used to manage a systems development project. It should be

Exhibit S2.2 The Five Maturity Levels of the Capability Maturity Model (CMM)

1. *Initial.* The software process is characterized as ad hoc, and occasionally even chaotic. Few processes are defined, and success depends on individual effort and heroics.

2. *Repeatable.* Basic project management processes are established to track cost, schedule, and functionality. The necessary process discipline is in place to repeat earlier successes on projects with similar applications.

3. *Defined.* The software process for both management and engineering activities is documented, standardized, and integrated into a standard software process for the organization. All projects use an approved, tailored version of the organization's standard software process for developing and maintaining software.

4. *Managed.* Detailed measures of the software process and product quality are collected. Both the software process and products are quantitatively understood and controlled.

5. *Optimizing.* Continuous process improvement is enabled by quantitative feedback from the process and from piloting innovative ideas and technologies.

Source: Carnegie Mellon Software Engineering Institute, "Capability Maturity Model® (SW-CMM®) for Software," http://www.sei.cmu.edu/activities/cmm/cmm.sum.html, May 11, 2001.

used when information systems are developed, acquired, or maintained. Exhibit S2.3 describes characteristics of an SDLC. Following such a methodology as well as the processes recommended in ISO 9000-3 and the SW-CMM should ensure that development efforts are efficient and consistently lead to information systems that meet organizational needs. These guidelines should be followed whether an organization is going to acquire an AIS (Chapter S1) or develop it in-house.

Exhibit S2.3 Characteristics of a Systems Development Methodology

- The project is divided into a number of identifiable processes, each having a starting and ending point. Each process comprises several activities, one or more *deliverables*, and several *management control points*. The division of the project into these small, manageable steps facilitates both project planning and project control.

- Specific reports and other documentation, called **deliverables**, must be produced periodically during systems development to make development personnel accountable for faithful execution of systems development tasks. An organization monitors the development process by reviewing the deliverables that are prepared at the end of each key step. Many organizations rely on this documentation for training new employees; it also provides users with a reference while they are operating the system.

- Users, managers, and auditors are required to participate in the project. These people generally provide approvals, often called *signoffs*, at preestablished management control points. **Signoffs** signify approval of the development process and the system being developed.

- The system must be tested thoroughly prior to implementation to ensure that it meets users' needs.

- A training plan is developed for those who will operate and use the new system.

- Formal program change controls (see Chapter 8) are established to preclude unauthorized changes to computer programs.

- A post-implementation review of all developed systems must be performed to assess the effectiveness and efficiency of the new system and of the development process.

Figure S2.1 presents the systems development life cycle to which we will refer in this and the next two chapters of this supplement. The right side of the figure depicts the four *development phases*: systems analysis, systems design, systems implementation, and

Figure S2.1 Systems Development Life Cycle

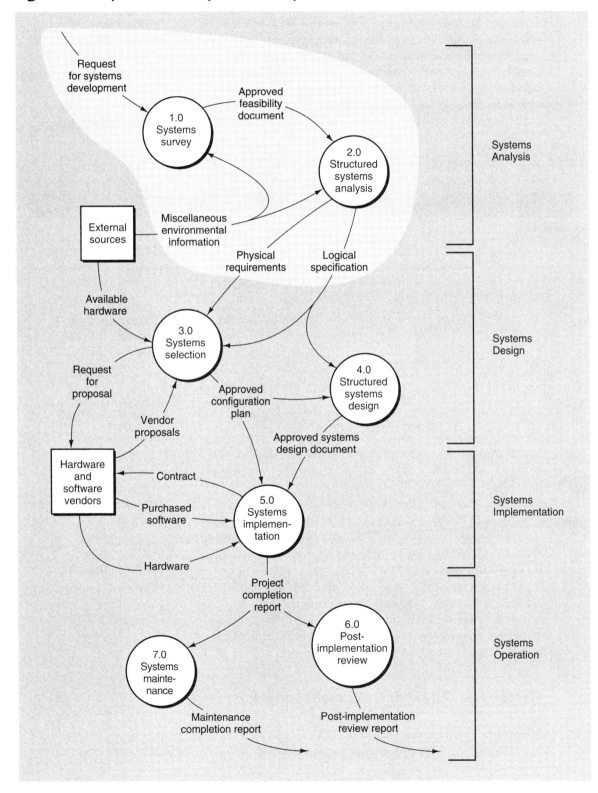

systems operation. The bubbles in Figure S2.1 identify the seven *development steps* undertaken to complete the four phases of development. Arrows flowing into each bubble represent the inputs needed to perform that step, whereas outward-flowing arrows represent the product of a step. A development process may not necessarily proceed *sequentially* through these steps. Rather, steps may be performed iteratively, out of sequence, or not at all. Table S2.1 lists the key purposes and tasks associated with the seven development steps (bubbles) shown in Figure S2.1. You should take some time now to review both the table and the figure. In this chapter, we will focus on the first phase of the SDLC—systems analysis.

Table S2.1 Information Systems Development Phases, Purposes, and Tasks*

Phase	Purpose	Tasks
Analysis (bubbles 1.0 and 2.0)	Develop specifications for a new or revised system.	Study the problem and the problem's environment. Propose alternative problem solutions.
Design (bubbles 3.0 and 4.0)	Develop an appropriate system manifestation.	Convert the logical solution into a physical design. Choose software and hardware. Write the detailed design specifications. Devise implementation plans, system tests, and training programs.
Implementation (bubble 5.0)	Begin using the new system.	Write, test, and debug the computer programs. Convert to new or revised system.
Operation (bubbles 6.0 and 7.0)	Use the new system.	Conduct post-implementation review. Perform systems maintenance.

* Refers to Figure S2.1.

E-BUSINESS   In the past, it often took years for a new system to move through the initial steps in the life cycle (i.e., bubbles 1.0 through 5.0 in Figure S2.1). Now organizations move at "Internet speed" and must develop business-to-business and other e-Business infrastructures in 90 to 180 days. If they do not, they may go out of business or be absorbed by those organizations that can.[1] Oftentimes, new systems development projects involve changes in the way a company operates. Such changes coupled with a need for speed raises the stakes regarding the odds of successfully accomplishing the systems development objectives mentioned earlier—especially if the business process changes are radical in nature, as discussed next.

BUSINESS PROCESS REENGINEERING

Business process reengineering is an activity larger in scope than systems development, as it addresses all of the processes in the organization, including the information systems

[1] Peter G. W. Keen, "Six Months—Or Else" *Computerworld* (April 10, 2000): 48.

processes. The principles described in this section might be considered the SDLC for development of organizational processes.

Rapid developments in the capabilities and applications of IT, such as e-Business, present organizations with increasingly difficult business opportunities and/or challenges. Managers are being asked to—sometimes being forced in order to ensure their companies' very survival—abandon long-held business beliefs and assumptions, rethink what they are attempting to accomplish, and analyze how they are trying to accomplish it. Business process reengineering (BPR) has been likened to presenting an organization's management with a blank piece of paper and asking it to reinvent all of the organization's processes from scratch. Why would management ever be motivated to engage in such an undertaking? In many cases, it has no alternative. Experiencing the harsh realities of an increasingly competitive environment, management recognizes that its companies must make mega-changes in how they operate or face extinction.

E-BUSINESS

Business process reengineering (BPR) (or simply *reengineering*) reflects a *fundamental* and oftentimes *radical* redesign of existing business *processes*. The motive is to successfully achieve *remarkable* improvements in the performance of an organization, both qualitative and quantitative. Let us emphasize four BPR concepts:

1. *Fundamental* rethinking of business processes requires management to challenge the very basic assumptions under which it operates and to ask such rudimentary questions as "Why do we do what we do?" and "Why do we do it the way we do it?" Without fundamental rethinking, technology has been used to automate old ways of doing business. The result is that what was a lousy way of doing a job became simply a faster, lousy way of doing the job.

2. *Radical* redesign relies on a fresh-start, clean-slate approach to examining an organization's business processes. This approach focuses on answers to the question, "If we were a brand new business, how would we operate our company?" The goal is to reinvent what is done and how it is done rather than to "tinker" with the present system by making marginal, incremental, superficial improvements to what is already being done. Achieving the goal requires forward-looking, creative thinkers who are unconstrained by what now exists.

3. Reengineering focuses on end-to-end business *processes* rather than on the individual activities that comprise the processes. BPR takes a holistic view of a business process as comprising a string of activities that cuts across traditional departmental or functional lines. BPR is concerned with the results of the process (i.e., with those activities that add value to the process).

4. Achieving *remarkable* improvements in performance measurements is related to the preceding two elements. The fundamental rethinking and radical redesign of business processes are aimed toward making quantum leaps in performance, however measured. These improvements are not in quality or speed, which often can be accomplished with marginal, incremental changes to existing processes. Reengineering, on the other hand, has much loftier objectives. For example, the Ford Motor Company reengineered their procurement process and reduced the number of persons employed in the process by 75 percent.[2]

A major manifestation of reengineering is that walls that surround separate functions and departments are obliterated. For instance, rather than order-taking, picking,

---

[2] Michael Hammer, "Reengineering Work: Don't Automate, Obliterate," *Harvard Business Review* (July–August 1990): 105–107.

shipping, and so forth, the entire process of order fulfillment is examined and those activities that add value for the customer are analyzed. Instead of assigning responsibility for these activities to multiple individuals and organizational units, one individual might be assigned to oversee them all. And, just as important, the measurement of performance might be changed from the number of orders processed by each individual to an assessment of customer service indicators such as delivering the right goods in the proper quantities, in satisfactory condition, and at the agreed-upon time and price. Perhaps you can see why systems development projects that simultaneously involve BPR are high risk ventures. But, if successful, the competitive advantage gained can be amazing. Exhibit S2.4 offers some guidance as to how to make BPR successful. An important consideration in all systems development projects, which is amplified when BPR is involved, deals with how to handle the human side of the equation. We take a quick look at this topic next.

CHANGE MANAGEMENT

The modern business organization lives or dies by its ability to respond to change. It must internalize a spirit of adaptation. However, most humans resist change. The introduction or modification of an information system is one of the most far-reaching changes that an organization can undergo, especially when these changes are accompanied by, or driven by, business process changes. To reap the full benefits of a new system, management must find ways to overcome the dysfunctional behaviors brought on by the implementation of a new information system. Experience has shown that resistance to change can be the foremost obstacle facing successful system implementation.

People's concerns regarding IT and business process changes have been with the actual and perceived changes in work procedures and relationships, corporate culture, and organizational hierarchy that these changes bring. To address these fears, the systems professional and the users must collaborate in the design and implementation of the new system. This collaboration must include the system itself and the process that will be followed during its development and installation. The change must be managed, but not directed. Rather, users must participate in the development and change processes.

ENTERPRISE SYSTEMS Research and practice provide guidance to help achieve successful change. A recent research study found that users who effectively participated in a systems change process were able to affect outcomes and had a more positive attitude about, and a higher involvement with, the new system. The system was also more successful.[3] In practice, successful, large IT change projects—especially those involving *enterprise systems*—must be driven by the business processes and managed by the business process owners. In these cases IT assists with, but does not drive, the change process.

Technological change will not be welcomed if it comes as a surprise. Users at all levels must be brought into the process early in the SDLC to encourage suggestions and discussion of the change. Users involved from the start and given a say in redesigning their jobs will tend to identify with the system. As problems arise, their attitude is more likely to be, "*We* have a problem," rather than, "The system makes too many mistakes."

---

[3] James E. Hunton and Jesse D. Beeler, "Effects of User Participation in Systems Development: A Longitudinal Field Experiment," *MIS Quarterly* (December 1997): 359–383.

Exhibit S2.4 Making BPR Successful

- *Organize around outcomes, not tasks.* This principle argues that we should have one person perform all the steps in a process; design the job around an objective or outcome rather than a single task. For example, a customer service representative might manage all the customer sales activities. As a result, one person is responsible for getting the item to the customer and for answering customer questions during the process. Two complementary means by which we improve outcomes are (1) determine what activities or tasks are needed to achieve the outcome and to *eliminate nonvalue-added activities* and (2) *create parallel activities* wherever possible. For example, the insurance and loan application processes often involve activities and decisions by multiple functions. By making use of shared databases, *image processing*, and intelligent workflow software, many activities can be accomplished simultaneously, thus improving output timeliness.

- *Have those who need the results of a process perform the process.* In exchange for the promise of more timely repairs, an electronic equipment manufacturer asked its customers to perform some of their own routine repairs and to carry the spare parts inventory required for their own machines. Now, customers make some repairs themselves using spare parts stored on site. The field service representatives, who had been making all repairs, answer customer calls and guide customers through a repair process using a diagnosis support system (an *expert system*). A computerized inventory management system monitors the spare parts inventories. Field service representatives are dispatched only for complex problems. The electronics manufacturer achieved better customer service and lower inventory carrying costs.

- *Integrate the processing of information into the work process that produces the information.* After the Ford Motor Company reengineered its procurement processes, the receiving department—and the receiving system—produced and processed information about the goods received instead of sending it to accounts payable. The receiving system compared the goods received with the order and took appropriate action (send the goods back or create a payable).

- *Treat geographically dispersed resources as though they were centralized.* Decentralized resources typically provide better service to their customers at the expense of creating redundant operations and lost economies of scale. At Hewlett-Packard, 50 decentralized purchasing functions provided excellent responsiveness and service to the plants but prevented H-P from benefiting from quantity discounts. After reengineering, H-P has a centralized purchasing function that creates and maintains a centralized database of vendors with whom they have negotiated contracts. Decentralized units can access the database to execute their own purchase orders.

- *Link parallel activities instead of integrating their results.* If parallel activities have been created, use communications networks, shared databases, and teleconferencing to coordinate activities that must eventually come together. For example, in the loan application process, decisions by one function that will affect the loan decision must be immediately communicated to other functions.

- *Put the decision point where the work is performed, and build controls into the process.* We can reduce nonvalue-added management and flatten the organization structure if we use information technology to capture and store data and *expert systems* to supply knowledge to enable people to make their own decisions. This changes the role of manager from controller and supervisor to supporter and facilitator.

- *Capture information once and at the source.* Collect and store data in online databases for all who need them. This principle is facilitated by information technology, such as telecommunications, networking, client/server architecture, EDI, image processing, relational database systems, bar coding, and intelligent workflow software.

In engineering a systems change, it is crucial to consider the human element. Resistance should be anticipated and its underlying causes addressed. User commitment can be enlisted by encouraging participation during development and by using achievement of business objectives, rather than IT change, to drive the process. Potential users must be sold on the benefits of a system and made to believe that they are capable of working with that system. A policy of coercion will lead to substandard performance.

ACCOUNTANT'S INVOLVEMENT IN SYSTEMS DEVELOPMENT

The focus here is on users *participating* in systems development rather than *conducting* systems development. That is, our intention is not to educate you as a systems analyst or designer, but to give you enough information to allow you to participate effectively in systems development projects. Your study of this chapter will allow you to solve simple systems analysis and design problems. Perhaps you are asking yourself, "I am not a computer programmer, so how can I participate in developing an IS?" Table S1.2 (page 9) indicates the ways accountants can become involved in AIS acquisitions. Most accountants are uniquely qualified also to participate in the broader category of systems development because they:

CONTROLS
- May be among the few people in an organization who can combine knowledge of IT, business, accounting, and internal control, as well as behavior and communications, to ensure that new systems meet the needs of the user and possess adequate internal controls.

- Have specialized skills, such as accounting and auditing, that can be applied to the development project. For example, an accountant might perform the analysis of a proposed system's costs, benefits, and internal controls.

- Possess a broad understanding of an organization's business processes. In the bulk of contemporary systems development projects the engineering of business processes drives the use of IT, not vice versa.

Because you are acquiring specialized skill and knowledge in accounting, IT, core business processes, project management, and auditing, among other valuable intellectual human and technical resources, you will be in a unique position to evaluate the systems development process and the systems being developed. Next, we will focus on two steps comprising the systems analysis phase of the SDLC—systems survey and structured systems analysis (see Figure S2.1, page 39).

SYSTEMS SURVEY

In this section we briefly discuss the systems survey—the first step in the development of a *particular* system. Our brevity is driven by the remarkable similarity between the systems survey in this chapter and the preliminary survey associated with acquiring an AIS, which was covered in Chapter S1. The similarity arises because whether you are acquiring a system from an external vendor or developing your own system, the first step in the analysis phase is nearly identical. Thus, where the same issues arise, we will briefly describe them here rather than duplicating material already covered.

Recall that *strategic planning* for the information systems function precedes and pervades *all* systems development. The systems survey is conducted to investigate information systems problems and to decide on a course of action. One course of action will be to proceed with development. However, during this initial investigation we may find that there is no problem and broader analysis is not warranted. We must be careful in reaching premature conclusions, because problems may be ill defined and not appropriately identified by the user.

Systems Survey Definition and Goals

The **systems survey**, often called a **feasibility study** or **preliminary feasibility study**, is a set of procedures conducted to determine the feasibility of a potential systems development project and to prepare a systems development plan for projects considered feasible. Refer to Figure S2.1 (page 39) to see the systems survey's place in the SDLC (bubble 1.0), its inputs (request for systems development and miscellaneous environmental information), and its outputs (approved feasibility document).

Each step in the SDLC has goals that support the systems development objectives (to develop information systems that satisfy the organization's needs and to develop information systems efficiently and effectively). An organization conducts a systems survey to determine, as *quickly* and as *inexpensively* as possible, whether it is worthwhile to proceed with subsequent development steps. Therefore, the *systems survey goals* are as follows:

- *Determine the nature and the extent of each reported problem.* For instance, if the sales department reports a problem of late deliveries, we want to know whether deliveries really are late, whether there are delays within the organization, or whether our sales personnel are promising unrealistic delivery dates.

- *Determine the scope of the problem.* For example, is a reported purchasing problem confined to the purchasing process, or is there a broader problem requiring more extensive analysis?

- *Propose a course of action that might solve the problem.* For example, propose systems development of the purchasing process to correct a purchasing problem.

- *Determine the feasibility of any proposed development.* Is there a *technically, operationally*, and *economically* feasible solution to the problem? For example, does computer technology exist to solve the problem (technical feasibility), is the organization ready to accept the new solution (operational feasibility), are the payback and internal rate of return estimates sufficient to allow the development project to proceed (economic feasibility)?

- *Devise a detailed plan for conducting the analysis step.* Determine who will conduct the analysis, who will head the project team, what tasks are required, and what the development timetable is.

- *Develop a summary plan for the entire development project.* For example, when will the system be implemented?

Systems Survey Tasks and Documents

Figure S2.2 (page 46) illustrates a lower-level view of process number 1.0 in Figure S2.1 (page 39) and outlines the *systems survey tasks and documents* necessary to achieve the systems survey goals. Next, we discuss the tasks associated with the systems survey (bubbles 1.1 through 1.4).

First, one or more persons makes a request for systems development. Such requests can arise from many sources, such as users, managers, auditors, and information systems personnel. The request should be made in a prescribed format and approved by one or more authorized persons. The approval process is designed to stop spurious or baseless requests from entering the first step of the systems survey—fact gathering (bubble 1.1).

Figure S2.2 **Systems Survey Tasks and Documents**

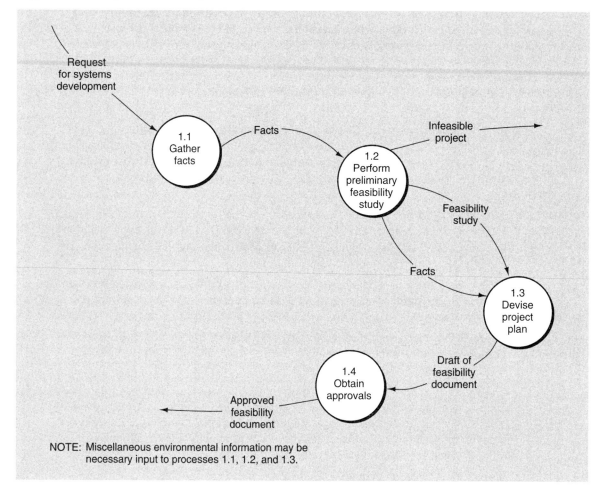

NOTE: Miscellaneous environmental information may be necessary input to processes 1.1, 1.2, and 1.3.

As discussed in Chapter S1, we gather facts mainly to determine if a problem exists, refine the nature of the problem, and determine the scope of the problem. This step is quite cursory; thus, it can and should be accomplished relatively quickly and inexpensively. If the analyst team determines that a probable case for a systems development project exists, the next step is to perform a preliminary feasibility study (bubble 1.2).

The three main objectives of conducting a feasibility study are to determine technical, operational, and economic feasibilities. This is one of the critical junctures in the SDLC, because if the proposed project passes these hurdles and is approved for further development (subject to available funds), the development costs begin to rise exponentially. Hence, the analysis team needs to be very careful in determining which projects are feasible.

The next step in the systems survey is to devise a project plan (bubble 1.3). The project plan basically outlines the project scope, identifies required resources, estimates various time demands and constraints, and quantifies (first approximation) the anticipated project costs. Once the project plan has been crafted, the documentation becomes known as the feasibility document, which needs to be approved (bubble 1.4).

This step involves obtaining user/participant approvals and management control point approvals. One cannot underestimate the importance of gaining the consent of all affected parties at this point in the development project, because their continued cooperation will be critical as the project progresses. Approvals of the feasibility document signify that the proposed development process and system are ready to go to the next step in the systems analysis phase—structured systems analysis (see bubble 2.0, Figure S2.1, page 39).

STRUCTURED SYSTEMS ANALYSIS

So that we can understand systems analysis, we will again compare systems development to building an industrial park. The architect's role for the industrial park is analogous to the analyst's role for systems development. In the preliminary stages of the industrial park project, the architect learns the general purpose of the industrial park (light manufacturing, warehousing, etc.). He also learns the approximate number of buildings and the size of each. From that information, the architect sketches a proposed park. From that sketch and the accompanying general specifications, estimated costs, and estimated schedule, the developer decides whether to proceed with the proposed project. This process is similar to that followed in the systems survey, with the systems analyst assuming the architect's role and the organization's management (or the *IT steering committee*) replacing the developer.

If the developer approves the continuation of the project, the architect must conduct a *detailed* study to determine each building's specific use, required room sizes, electrical and plumbing requirements, floor load weights, private versus public areas, number of personnel who will occupy the completed buildings, technical requirements, and so on. During this detailed study, the architect develops a *functional* model of the proposed project. The detailed study by the architect is similar to systems analysis, and the logical specification (one of the outputs of the analysis step) is the model for the new system.

Systems Analysis Definition and Goals

Structured systems analysis reflects a set of procedures conducted to generate the *specifications* for a new (or modified) information system or subsystem. Systems analysis is often called *structured systems analysis* when certain structured tools and techniques, such as data flow diagrams (DFDs), are used in conducting the analysis. To simplify our discussions, we will refer to structured systems analysis as simply systems analysis.

The *systems analysis goals* are as follows:

- *Define the problem precisely.* In the systems survey, we verified that there was a problem and determined the problem's sources. In systems analysis, we want to know and understand the problem in enough detail to solve it.

- *Devise alternative designs (solutions).* There is always more than one way to solve a problem or to design a system, and we want to develop several solutions from which to choose.

- *Choose and justify one of these alternative design solutions.* One solution must be chosen, and the choice should be justified using cost/effectiveness analysis or some other criterion, such as political or legal considerations (e.g., government reporting requirements).

- *Develop logical specifications for the selected design.* These detailed specifications are used to design the new system.

- *Develop the physical requirements for the selected design.* For example, we want to define requirements such as the amount of data to be stored, functional layouts for computer inquiry screens and reports, and processing response times, which lead to equipment requirements. There can be several alternative physical designs for each logical requirement.

- *Develop the budget for the next two systems development phases (systems design, Chapter S3, and systems implementation, Chapter S4).* These budgets are critical in determining development costs and controlling later development activities.

The logical specifications and physical requirements become the criteria by which the user will accept the new or modified system. The better we perform systems analysis, the more likely that the system will meet user requirements and become accepted, implemented, and used effectively.

ENTERPRISE SYSTEMS   It is imperative to perform a top-quality analysis when introducing an *enterprise system*. It is during the analysis step that we model the business processes and determine the process changes that will be required. These changes must be understood and accepted by the business process owners and system users for successful implementation. Otherwise there will be strong resistance to the implementation and that will lead to the failure of the new system. In an enterprise systems implementation, business process changes must be made to fit the enterprise system's processes.

E-BUSINESS   Determination of user requirements in the analysis step can be more difficult in an e-Business implementation. In such an implementation, we must determine user requirements inside *and outside* the organization. We must consider the functional needs of customers and business partners, as well as any requirements for infrastructure to connect our internal systems to the outside users (e.g., customer, business partners).

Systems Analysis Tasks and Documents

Figure S2.3 reflects a lower-level view of process 2.0 in Figure S2.1 (page 39) and outlines the *systems analysis tasks and documents* necessary to achieve the *systems analysis goals*. Systems analysis begins with an *approved feasibility document* and ends with *physical requirements, a budget and schedule*, and *a logical specification*. Because the budget and schedule arise from each systems development step, they are not shown as separate outputs. We discuss next each of the systems analysis tasks, starting with the output (the analysis deliverable), then the input (triggering the systems analysis), and finally the intermediate tasks (bubbles 2.1 through 2.6).

The Analysis Deliverable: The Approved Systems Analysis Document

Figure S2.3 has two outputs: the **logical specification** and the **physical requirements**. There are also the implied, but not shown, budget and schedule. All three systems analysis outputs are generally part of a single **approved systems analysis document**—the final output of systems analysis. Exhibit S2.5 (page 50) outlines the contents of this document. The logical specification consists of all items except those designated as the budget and schedule (part 7) and the physical requirements (part 8). An understanding of the information collected and included in the approved systems analysis document will help you understand the steps that an analyst must perform *during* the systems analysis.

Triggering Systems Analysis

If the organization's management (or *IT steering committee*) approves the project for further systems development, systems analysis follows the systems survey. Management

Figure S2.3 **Systems Analysis Tasks and Documents**

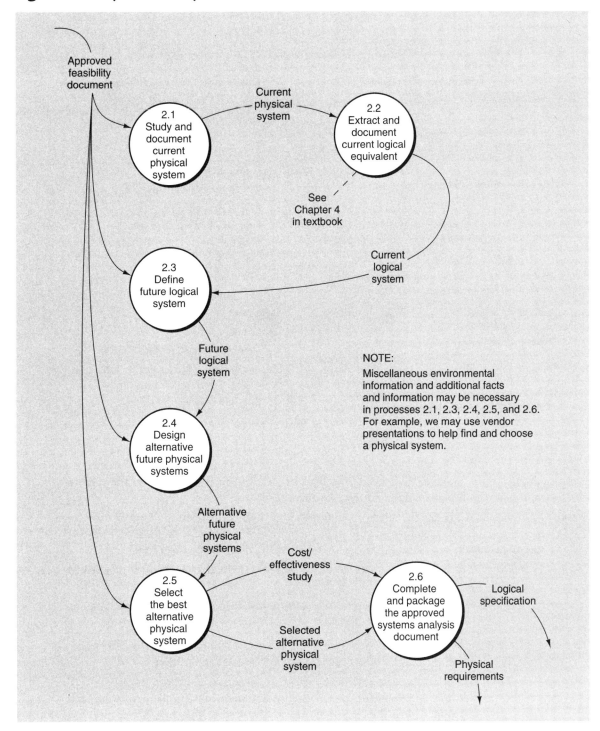

bases the decision to proceed on the *approved feasibility document* and other information. Management might decide to reduce the suggested analysis scope in order to reduce the short-term development costs. Or, management might cancel, postpone, or

Exhibit S2.5 Typical Contents of an Approved Systems Analysis Document

1. **Executive summary**
   a. Project summary
   b. Summary of proposed system
   c. Summary of impact of new system
   d. Summary of cost/effectiveness and recommendations

2. **Systems analysis summary**
   Summary of the facts gathered and analysis performed

3. **User requirements for the new system**
   a. Operating requirements
   b. Information requirements
   c. Control requirements

4. **Logical specifications for the new system**
   a. Data flow diagrams and narrative describing the new logical system
   b. Summary of improvements brought about by new logical design (effectiveness)

5. **Description of future physical system**
   a. Data flow diagrams, flowcharts, and narrative describing the new physical system
   b. Summary of cost/benefit improvements brought about by the new physical system

6. **New system constraints**
   a. Hardware and software constraints
   b. Interface constraints
   c. Contractual and legal requirements

7. **Design phase budget and schedule**
   a. Design phase personnel and computer requirements
   b. Development schedule

8. **Physical requirements**
   a. Workload and volume
   b. Response times
   c. Functional layouts of computer inquiry screens and reports
   d. System growth

9. **Recommendations**
   Project leader's recommendations

10. **Approvals**

11. **Attachments**
    a. Approved feasibility document
    b. Analysis memos, summaries, tables, graphs, charts
    c. Cost/effectiveness schedules

modify future systems work because a major modification is preferred to the maintenance approach being suggested (or vice versa).

ENTERPRISE SYSTEMS   Figure S2.4 depicts the alternatives considered by Boston Scientific Corporation before they embarked on a worldwide implementation of SAP R/3. In addition to the alternative chosen—to standardize on SAP R/3 worldwide—they considered:

- *Interfaces*: Build interfaces among the many systems that existed at their worldwide affiliates.

- *Standardize on one*: Implement at all of the worldwide affiliates the set of applications in use at one of those affiliates.

- *Build it*: Build their own system and write the necessary applications software.

- *Best of breed*: Select the best system available for each application.

- *EBS (Enterprise Business Solution)*: Select an integrated software package (*ERP*) to provide the processing functionality for all applications. Implement that package worldwide. This is the SAP solution.

The development options in Figure S2.4 are typical of the choices from which organizations may choose. In the systems survey we begin to get some sense of these alternatives and which one looks best for us at this time. In the analysis step of systems devel-

Figure S2.4 Development Choices at Boston Scientific

Alternatives Considered

Judgment Criteria:	Interface	Standardize on One	Build It	Best of Breed	EBS
• Risk to create solution	LOW	MED	HIGH	MED	MED
• Length of overall implementation	SHORT	MED	LONG	LONG	MED
• Business functionality	WORST	WORST	BEST	BEST	BEST
• Supports common solution goal	WORST	BEST	BEST	MED	BEST
• Overall cost; project	LEAST	MED	MOST	MOST	MED
• IT support infrastructure (people)	MED	LEAST	MOST	MOST	LEAST
• Long-term solution viability	WORST	WORST	MED	MED	BEST
• Business, resource requirements	LEAST	MED	MOST	MOST	MOST

Source: Reprinted with permission from Dave Ellard, Vice President, Global Systems, Boston Scientific Corporation.

opment, we must examine each alternative and gather enough information to make a choice and to proceed with development along one of the alternative paths.

Study and Document the Current Physical System

The first step the analysis team performs is to *study and document the current physical system.* (see Figure S2.3, page 49). The team reads and interprets existing documentation, such as data flow diagrams and systems flowcharts, corrects that documentation as needed or prepares new documentation. Chapter 4 in the textbook helps you develop the skills necessary for this step. The team wants to build on the information available in the *approved feasibility document* and understand completely the current system operations. Given the system's goals, what should the system be doing? Should the order entry system be supporting customer inquiries? For what reason is the system operating as it is? Why are there errors?

In the systems survey step, the analyst develops *general* information about the prospective system. Regarding the systems analysis step, the analyst first verifies the accuracy and reasonableness of the information already gathered. Then the analysis team solidifies its understanding of the existing system by gathering, analyzing, and *documenting* additional information. The analysts need the additional information to specify the new system *in detail.*

After studying the current physical environment (gathering and analyzing facts), the analysis team completes the analysis documentation. It is a little misleading to say that the analysts do not complete the documentation until *after* they gather and analyze information. The analysis team prepares documentation *during* the entire analysis. Systems analysis documentation includes memos summarizing interviews and observations, charts, tables, and graphs, completed questionnaires (or summaries of results), flowcharts, physical data flow diagrams, and organization charts.

Extract and Document the Current Logical Equivalent

Having studied and documented the current physical system,[4] what does the analyst do next? He might proceed in any one of three directions.

1. Having as a goal the future physical system and being unconcerned about how to get to that new system, users would like the analyst to leap immediately to the future physical system (bubble 2.4 in Figure S2.3, page 49). The users, unfortunately, do not have a clear idea of what the new system should be, and vague ideas are not an adequate basis for design and implementation.

2. The analyst, concerned with design features, alternative implementations, and the costs and benefits of those alternatives, would like to start with the future logical system (bubble 2.3 in Figure S2.3).

3. A third alternative, following the steps in Figure S2.3, lead to successful development efforts:
    *   Study the current physical system (bubble 2.1).
    *   Document the current logical system (bubble 2.2).
    *   Define the future logical system (bubble 2.3).
    *   Design the future physical system (bubble 2.4).

To start deriving the current logical equivalent, the analyst removes all the physical elements from the *current physical data flow diagram* and produces a *current logical data flow diagram*, which reflects a description of the current logical system. Again, you learned these skills in textbook Chapter 4.

Figure S2.5 is the Causeway current logical DFD. Exhibit S2.6 (page 54) is the narrative description of that system. Because we will use the Causeway system as an example in this chapter, you should review both the figure and the exhibit before proceeding.

Define Future Logical System

One of the most important, and most problematic, tasks in the systems analysis step is to define user requirements for the new/modified system. It also may be necessary to rank those requirements in order of importance in the event that resources or other constraints make it impossible to satisfy all user requirements. One expert proposes that user requirements be placed in three categories. The first are critical features without which the system would be unusable and rejected by the users. The second category includes those features without which the users would be greatly affected but still willing to use the system. The third category includes those features that users would love to have but would not miss if they were not available.[5] Recall the discussion from Chapter S1 of critical (i.e., level 9) through nice-to-have (i.e., level 1) needs that were used when entering software requirements into *The Accounting Library*.

For the sake of discussion, let us assume that we have completed our investigation and have determined that Causeway has several objectives in mind in reengineering their cash receipts system. For the customers Causeway wants to achieve a greater degree of flexibility and customer service. Causeway also wants to lower costs for the customers and themselves as well as accelerate their cash flows. The customers want to use innovative and efficient processes in conducting business with Causeway. The customers also

---

[4] Actually, many development projects have proceeded without documenting the current physical environment. Either there was *no existing* system, or the analysts considered documenting the current physical system too costly.

[5] Ed Yourdon, "The Value of Triage," *Computerworld* (March 20, 2000): 40.

Figure S2.5 Causeway Current Logical System

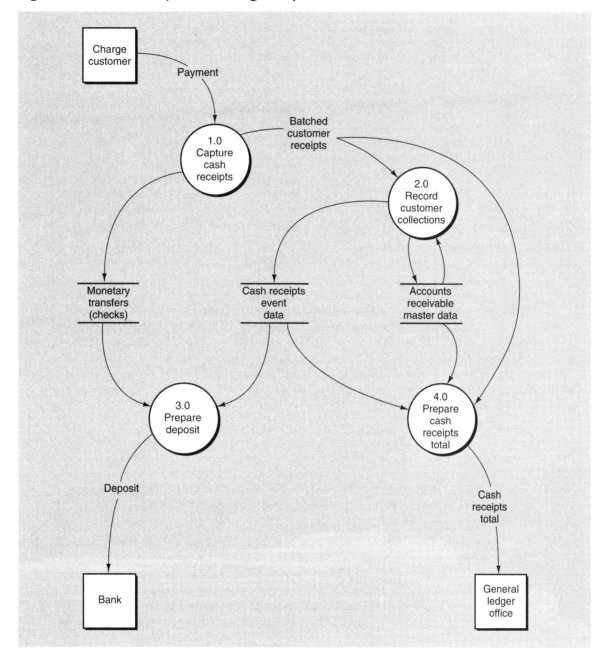

want instant access to information about their accounts receivable balances. Finally, Causeway wants to take advantage of current technology, such as the Internet. In fact, as a result of the analysis, it was determined that Causeway would now permit its customers to receive bills and make payments electronically using an electronic bill presentment and payment system.[6]

---

[6] See textbook Chapter 11 for a discussion of electronic bill presentment and payment systems.

Exhibit S2.6 Causeway Company System Narrative

The Causeway Company uses the following procedures to process the cash received from credit sales. Customers send checks and remittance advices to Causeway. The mailroom clerk at Causeway endorses the checks and writes the amount paid and the check number on the remittance advice. Periodically, the mailroom clerk prepares a batch total of the remittance advices and sends the batch of remittance advices to accounts receivable, along with a copy of the batch total. At the same time, the clerk sends the corresponding batch of checks to the cashier.

In accounts receivable, a clerk enters the batch into the computer by keying the batch total, the customer number, the invoice number, the amount paid, and the check number. After verifying that the invoice is open and that the correct amount is being paid, the computer updates the accounts receivable master data. If there are any discrepancies, the clerk is notified.

At the end of each batch (or at the end of the day), the computer prints a deposit slip in duplicate on the printer in the cashier's office. The cashier compares the deposit slip to the corresponding batch of checks and then takes the deposit to the bank.

As they are entered, the check number and the amount paid for each receipt are logged on a disk. This event data is used to create a cash receipts listing at the end of each day. A summary of customer accounts paid that day is also printed at this time. The accounts receivable clerk compares these reports to the remittance advices and batch totals and sends the total of the cash receipts to the general ledger office.

Working with the current logical system (Figure S2.5, page 53), Causeway modeled the future logical system from Figure S2.6. Examine these figures to see the differences between the two. Like the current logical DFD, the future logical DFD describes a system's logical features. However, unlike the current diagram, the future diagram describes what a system *will do* rather than what it *presently does*. Follow along with us as we discuss the three steps that are performed to derive a future logical system from a current logical DFD.

1. *Add new activities.* The first step in modeling the future logical system is to add processes to handle new events or to eliminate processes where an event has been eliminated. Examples of new events include reports, inquiries, and temporal events such as "reach reorder point" or "payment overdue." The system's goals should be a guide in determining such events and activities. For Causeway, the following processes were eliminated, new events defined, and processes added:

   • Activity 1.0 from Figure S2.5 has been radically altered, so much so that we consider it a new activity. In the new activity 1.0 (in Figure S2.6) the customer directly accesses her accounts receivable balance, selects the items and the amount to be paid, and authorizes a payment. Then, the third party that processes this payment for Causeway verifies they will be able to transfer the necessary funds from the customer's bank to Causeway's bank. The accounts receivable master data is updated to reflect that a payment has been authorized and that funds are due from the bank.

   • Bubble 3.0 (Figure S2.5) is no longer needed because the third-party payment processor will execute a funds transfer to the Causeway bank.

2. *Remodel existing activities.* The second step in modeling the future logical system is to redesign *existing* activities to make them more effective and efficient. Activities are remodeled to reduce redundancies, to eliminate activities not required, and to realign (combine or separate) activities to improve the system's logic. Again, the system goals should be the guide.

   • Bubble 2.0 still records the customer payment and updates the customer's accounts receivable balance to reflect that the payment has been received from the

Figure S2.6 Causeway Future Logical System

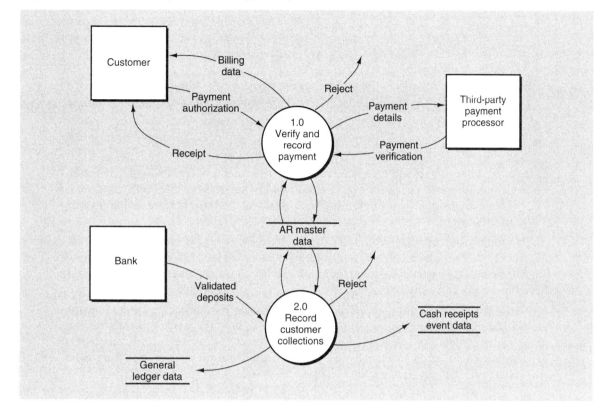

bank. However, this process is now triggered by data received from the bank, not the customer. This process also adds a record of the cash receipt to the cash receipts event data and updates the general ledger (cash, accounts receivable, cash discounts).

- The activities in bubble 4.0 in Figure S2.5 related to the general ledger update are combined with the activities in the new bubble 2.0 (Figure S2.6) that occur at the time that the customer collection is recorded.

3. *Add or change control activities.* Some controls are retained from the current system, either in their current form or with modification. Some controls—those found to be inefficient, redundant, or otherwise no longer needed—are eliminated. The following control activities are included in Figure S2.6, the future logical system: **CONTROLS**

- The first place where a control activity is desirable is within process 1.0. After reviewing the payment details (e.g., customer name, customer number, items and amount to be paid, bank, and bank account number), the third-party payment processor notifies Causeway that a payment transfer can be made. If Causeway does not receive this verification, a reject routine is initiated.

- The second place where a control activity is desirable is within process 2.0. To ensure the validity and accuracy of the payment data received from the bank, each payment is compared to the accounts receivable data. Payment data that does not agree with expected payments will be handled by an exception routine.

The development team may propose alternative future logical systems. Logical design alternatives include variations of the following:

- Activities
- Data stores
- Control activities

For example, *logical alternatives* to the system suggested by Figure S2.6 are:

1. Rather than presenting customers with all the details of their accounts receivable balances, some of that data could be extracted to a separate data store for use during payment processing. (This could also be accomplished by simply making less of the existing data available to the customers.)

2. In addition to providing customers with this method for making payments, Causeway could retain its previous method of processing customer payments. (Causeway would certainly do this. We have eliminated this option to simplify our presentation.)

To simplify the example, we will not use any of these *logical* alternatives. Therefore, Figure S2.6 is the only future logical system Causeway will use. Effectiveness analysis—an assessment of a particular design's potential ability to meet a system's goals—would have been used to choose the logical alternative to be implemented.

Notice that the alternative *logical* designs do not show *how* a procedure would be implemented. For example, Figure S2.6 does not tell us how the bank will transmit the data "validated deposits." Will the transmission be direct (i.e., computer to computer)? Will the bank send an EDI transmission or an e-mail? Until we choose the future *physical* system, we will not have answers to these questions.

Before moving on, let us compare for a moment the steps that we went through in Chapter S1 to purchase an AIS system, and the steps that we just went through here to build the new system in-house. As previously noted, the systems survey is very similar to the preliminary survey of Chapter S1. In both cases we are deciding if and how we should proceed with systems development. In fact, it is in this step that we might choose to buy or build the new system.

For the build in-house option, we proceeded to structured systems analysis in this chapter. Again, the process of developing the logical specifications and the physical requirements are very similar to the process followed in Chapter S1 to develop the approved AIS specifications. However, in Chapter S1 our logical and physical choices were constrained by the software packages available for purchase. Consequently, we spent less effort formally specifying our logical and physical requirements than we do here for an in-house system for which the specifications can be unique.

Design Alternative Future Physical Systems

We are now ready to describe *how* the new system will operate. Working with the future logical system shown in Figure S2.6, an analysis team could devise several *physical* alternatives. The following describes how the future physical system might be derived from the future logical system (Figure S2.6).

1. The first step in developing a future physical system is to decide which processes will be manual and which will be automated. For example, in Figure S2.6, bubble 1.0 *would* probably be partly manual and partly automated, and bubble 2.0 *could* be partly manual and partly automated.

2. As a second step in developing an alternative physical design, the analyst must decide which processes will begin immediately upon occurrence of an event and

which will operate only periodically (often with batches of business events data). For example, bubble 1.0 might contain steps that are completed in the *immediate* mode (i.e., processing begins as soon as the process's trigger, such as query request or payment authorization, is received from a customer), and bubble 2.0 might contain steps that are performed in the *periodic* mode (i.e., processing does not begin until a batch is completed or until a certain time is reached).

3. The final step in designing alternative physical systems is to complete specifications for the future physical system. Typically, specifications are written for each bubble in the future physical system. These specifications indicate how, where, and in what form inputs are processed and how, where, and in what form outputs are produced. Exhibit S2.7 contains the Causeway future physical system specifications. Review those specifications before proceeding.

Exhibit S2.7 Causeway Future Physical System Specifications

Assume that the following physical design specifications have been selected for the Causeway system:

Bubble 1.0. At the end of each billing cycle, Causeway customers are notified via e-mail that they have a new balance due (this is not shown in Figure S2.6 on page 55; it is part of the billing system). Customers log on to the Causeway payment Web site (i.e., the biller direct method), access their account, and decide what and how much to pay. The details of the payment, such as customer name, customer number, bank account number, and amount to be paid are sent to the third-party payment processor. They send back a verification that allows Causeway to reduce the receivable and notify the customer that the payment has been processed. Causeway records this payment in the accounts receivable master data.

At the third-party payment processor. When the third-party processor receives the payment details they determine if they have sufficient information and will be able to prepare a funds transfer. Causeway is notified of the results of this determination via the flow "payment verification." At the end of each day the third-party processor consolidates all payments made that day (by Causeway and other merchants) and prepares an ACH (Automated Clearing House) file containing all of the electronic funds transfers to be made to clear the day's payments. The file is submitted through the ACH network into the banking system. Each bank (including Causeway's) receives the transfers relevant to its customers. Causeway's bank makes the appropriate transfers and prepares a file to be sent to Causeway. The file contains a list of the customer payments (customer name, number, items paid, and amount). The bank sends this file to Causeway each evening.

Bubble 2.0. When the payment file is received from the bank, Causeway changes the accounts receivable data to reflect that an expected payment has been received. A record of the payment is recorded in the cash receipts event data and the general ledger data.

When specifying physical systems, we may choose from a host of alternatives. To keep the discussion simple, we will suggest just a few alternatives to the specifications for bubble 1.0 in Exhibit S2.7.

1. *Alternative technologies.* The current design assumes that Causeway will host its own bill payment site—the biller direct model. However, Causeway could make use of the services of a third party—such as CheckFree—to host the bill payment site. In this latter case, customers would log on to the third-party server to make their payments.

2. *Alternative modes.* The third-party payment processor and the bank could process individual payments in the *immediate* mode and send each on to Causeway for immediate processing (i.e., for recording to the accounts receivable master data, cash receipts data, and general ledger).

For simplicity in presenting our example, we will leave only two physical alternatives from which to choose. The two alternative designs that we have arbitrarily decided to consider further are:

1. Using the biller direct model specified in Exhibit S2.7.
2. Using a third party to host the payment Web site.

Select the Best Alternative Physical System

The analysis team, working with the new system's users, must now recommend the implementation of one of the alternative physical systems (bubble 2.5, Figure S2.3, page 49). The ultimate selection involves two decisions:

- The analysis team must decide which alternative system to recommend to the users and management.
- Given the analysis team's recommendation, the firm's management, usually the *IT steering committee*, must decide whether to undertake further development. And, if further development is chosen, management must decide which alternative system should be developed.

This two-part decision process is often an *iterative* process. The analysis team may recommend an alternative system and the users may disagree, thus requiring that the team rework its proposed system. After agreeing on the proposed system, the user/analyst team's proposal is forwarded for approval by the IT steering committee. This committee must decide whether the development effort justifies expenditure of the firm's cash. To reduce costs, for example, the IT steering committee may ask for revisions to the system, thus requiring yet another reworking of the proposed system.

If the users, management, and the IT steering committee have been keeping track of the analysis team's progress and have informed the team of all criteria appropriate for choosing development solutions, there should not be a disagreement between the team and the IT steering committee about which alternative is the best. Also, remember that the IT steering committee still maintains an option to make no change whatsoever to the system. This do nothing option becomes less likely to be chosen the further we progress with, and the more we spend on, the development of this system.

To facilitate selecting an alternative future physical system, the systems analysis team conducts a **cost/effectiveness study**, which provides quantitative and certain qualitative information concerning each of the alternatives. This information is used to decide which alternative best meets a user's needs. In making this determination, the team asks two questions. First, "Which alternative accomplishes the user's goals for the least cost (or greatest benefit)?" This question is addressed by the **cost/benefit study** (or **cost/benefit analysis**). Second, "Which alternative best accomplishes the user's goals for the system being developed?" This question is addressed by the **effectiveness study** (or **effectiveness analysis**).

Perform the Cost/Benefit Analysis. The cost/benefit analysis or study is performed first because the data are *relatively* easy to obtain and are more objective than the data on effectiveness. Also, for many decision makers and for many decisions, the cost/benefit criterion is the most important.

In conducting the cost/benefit study, the analyst first *estimates* the *costs* of the new system. Costs include **direct costs**, which are those directly attributable to the system or the system change. Examples of direct costs include equipment purchased, personnel salaries, site preparation, and materials and supplies. **Indirect costs** are not directly attributable to the system or the system change. Costs that we would normally associate with overhead expenses, such as personnel fringe benefits and utilities, are indirect costs.

A **tangible cost** is one that *can be reasonably quantified*, such as a software purchase and insurance. An **intangible cost** is one that *cannot be reasonably quantified*, such as productivity losses caused by low employee morale.

We incur **nonrecurring costs**, such as those for systems development, only once to get the system operational. **Recurring costs**, such as those for equipment rental, occur throughout all or most of the system's life.

Early in the development process, it may be difficult to estimate all costs. For example, hardware costs depend on decisions made in the next development phase, systems selection (see Chapter S3). The amount of intangible costs may never be known. What is important is to *identify* all costs. One such cost is that incurred by users participating in the development. Such costs should be, but seldom are, charged to the development project.

The second step in the cost/benefit study is to estimate benefits. The benefit categories are similar to those for cost. For example, benefits directly attributable to the system or the system change, such as reduced personnel and hardware costs and improved data reliability, are **direct benefits**.

Indirect benefits are not directly attributable to the system or the system change. For example, increased revenue may result from improving customer support. But normally we would not be able to determine how much of the increased revenue resulted from the system change. Or, reduced inventory carrying costs may result from system changes and from other changes in purchasing processes.

Tangible benefits are those that can be reasonably quantified, such as reduced equipment costs and increased revenues. **Intangible benefits**, such as those resulting from improved information, cannot be reasonably quantified. For example, a new system may improve control, but we may not be able to estimate the dollar benefits of the improved control with any satisfactory degree of certainty.

Intangible benefits take on increased importance as organizations develop a larger percentage of systems aimed at solving management and decision-making problems. Determining the benefits for the traditional "bread and butter" systems, such as payroll and accounts receivable, is relatively easy. The benefits for such systems usually include items such as reduced clerical costs. However, determining the benefits for a market analysis system presents problems. By how much will sales increase if we provide management with better information? In the cost/benefit analysis, we do our best to estimate costs and benefits. In the effectiveness analysis, we handle costs and benefits for which estimates were not possible.

Perform the Effectiveness Analysis. After conducting the cost/benefit analysis, the analysis team should determine each alternative's effectiveness. The ranking of each alternative on its relative ability to satisfy the user's requirements (goals) for the system either verifies the team's cost/benefit results or produces conflicting results. The effectiveness analysis might proceed as follows. The analysts and the user list all relevant criteria, including costs and benefits used in the cost/benefit analysis. It is at this time that we include intangible items for which monetary costs and benefits could not be estimated during the cost/benefit study. The users and the analysts jointly assign subjective rankings to each criterion for each alternative. The team then ranks the alternatives by summarizing the ratings.

The final step in selecting the alternative physical system is to recommend an alternative to the user, to management, and to the *IT steering committee*. Normally, making the recommendation is a straightforward process because the team recommends the highest ranking alternative. However, there may be conflicting information, as when one alternative ranks best in the cost/benefit analysis but another ranks best in the effectiveness analysis. In cases where one alternative is not clearly superior, the user and analysts must confer about and agree on an alternative to be proposed to the IT steering committee.[7] Usually, information about all alternatives, along with the development team's recommendation, is presented to the committee.

Let us summarize our discussion of the cost/effectiveness analyses. The criteria in the cost/effectiveness study are used to choose among alternative logical and physical designs and to decide how to allocate funds among competing development projects. The criteria also become the goals for the new system and the basis for the user's acceptance of the new system.

Complete and Package the Approved Systems Analysis Document

To complete the systems analysis, the project team must collect the products of the analysis and organize these products into the *approved systems analysis document* (see Exhibit S2.5, page 50 and Figure S2.3, bubble 2.6, page 49). Recall that the approved systems analysis document has two main components—the logical specification and the physical requirements (a third component, the budget and schedule, is implied). Each piece is "packaged" for the *chosen system alternative*. As a practical matter, some of this packaging might be deferred, pending approval by the IT steering committee. Let us discuss how each piece is packaged.

The first analysis deliverable is the logical specification. This is used in systems selection to choose the appropriate software to be acquired from external sources (as discussed in Chapter S1). Or, if the software is developed in-house (as assumed in this chapter), it is used in structured systems design to design the software and to develop manual procedures, training programs, and so on. The following logical specification items might be added or completed at this time:

- *Executive summary.* A DFD and narrative outlining the major features, objectives, benefits, and design constraints of the new system.
- *Process description.* A DFD and narrative for each process function. The narrative consists of a statement of the process's purpose, description of the work and data flow, user requirements, interface, and design constraints.
- *Information requirements.* For each input, output, and data store, we must describe the purpose, description, origin or source, major elements, frequency, volume, and distribution.
- *Miscellaneous functions.* Specifications for the following might be completed: editing, error checking, error messages, data maintenance, audit requirements, controls, security, and backup.

The second analysis deliverable is the *physical requirements*. These requirements are used in systems selection to acquire computer equipment for the new system. In addition to the physical requirements related to hardware, the physical requirements should include *functional* layouts of inquiry screens and reports. These are important for at least two reasons. First, users are as much concerned with how they will interface with

---

[7] Be aware that reaching such agreements can present practical problems that are beyond this text's scope. Suffice it to say that the "agreement" does not just magically happen.

the system as they are with the system's logic. Their information needs must be clearly and completely identified at this point in the development. Second, it is virtually impossible to perform a high-quality software study unless we can compare the outputs of proposed vendor systems to our specific requirements. At this point, the sample reports and screens are called *functional* layouts because they show the information elements that are needed without getting into all the *details* of the screen or report design, a topic that is covered in Chapter S4.

Another deliverable, implicit at the conclusion of each systems development step, is the *budget and schedule*, which contains two major parts:

1. The *budget*, obtained during the cost/benefit analysis, specifies the expected costs to complete the systems development.
2. *Schedules* control systems development efforts by setting limits on the time to be spent on development activities and by coordinating those activities.

The final step in completing and packaging the approved systems analysis document is to obtain approvals. As discussed earlier, *signoffs* may be obtained from users, information services, management, and internal auditors. In addition, the controller may sign off to indicate that the cost/benefit analysis is reasonable.

Summary

In this summary, we expand on the material presented in this chapter and show how it relates to your future careers in *accounting* and *auditing* by comparing systems analysis to auditing.

The initial auditing stages look very much like systems analysis. Although their goals differ, both auditors and analysts begin their work by documenting an existing system. Some documentation tools are common to auditing and systems analysis. In the initial audit stages the auditor gathers information to gain a general understanding of the system to be investigated during the audit. This process is not unlike the systems survey in that the auditor and the analyst will observe, interview, and gather and prepare documentation. In the systems survey, the analyst develops a plan for conducting systems development, called the *feasibility document*. The auditor develops a plan for conducting the audit, called the *audit program*.

In the next audit stage, the auditor gets an in-depth understanding of those system components that will be the subject of the audit. He gathers information using interviews, observations, and document review; also, he may administer questionnaires, usually internal control questionnaires. The auditor prepares working papers and *flowcharts* to document his work. Again, the procedures during the auditor's detailed review are similar to the analyst's work during systems analysis.

Although the *processes* appear to be similar, the analyst's and the auditor's *purposes* are different. The analyst wants to understand a system's problems so that she can propose solutions to those problems. The auditor wants to understand a system so that his audit plan will recognize the system's strengths and weaknesses. The auditor also wants to provide services in addition to the audit (value-added services). He can do so by gaining an understanding of his clients' systems and offering advice on how to improve them. As we have noted before, the Sarbanes-Oxley Act of 2002 limits the extent to which the auditor can provide consulting services, especially systems development consulting, to his audit clients. Still, the auditor wants to be a business advisor to his clients and to provide assistance to his clients while complying with Sarbanes-Oxley.

Review Questions

RQ S2-1 What is systems development?

RQ S2-2 What are the systems development objectives?

RQ S2-3 What are the five maturity levels of the Capability Maturity Model (CMM)?

RQ S2-4 What benefits are derived from using a systems development methodology?

RQ S2-5 What are the systems development phases and steps?

RQ S2-6 What are the key elements and principles of business process reengineering (BPR)?

RQ S2-7 Describe the ways that an accountant might be involved in systems development.

RQ S2-8 What are the systems survey goals?

RQ S2-9 Why do we obtain signoffs on the feasibility document?

RQ S2-10 What are the goals of structured systems analysis?

RQ S2-11 What is the purpose of each of the three main components of the approved systems analysis document (the logical specification, the budget and schedule, and the physical requirements)?

RQ S2-12 Why do we study and document the current physical environment?

RQ S2-13 Why do we develop a current logical model of an information system?

RQ S2-14 Why do we develop alternative logical designs?

RQ S2-15 Why do we develop alternative physical designs?

RQ S2-16 Why do we conduct a cost/benefit analysis?

RQ S2-17 Why do we conduct an effectiveness analysis?

RQ S2-18 Give examples of *direct* costs and benefits.

RQ S2-19 Give examples of *indirect* costs and benefits.

RQ S2-20 Give examples of *intangible* costs and benefits.

Discussion Questions

DQ S2-1 Give five examples of why one information system might experience more iterations of the SDLC than another information system (systems in different organizations or different application subsystems within one organization).

DQ S2-2 Discuss several factors affecting (negatively or positively) the achievement of systems development objectives.

DQ S2-3 "As long as we plan a systems development project and carry out the project in an orderly manner, we don't need a formal, documented systems development methodology." Do you agree? Discuss fully.

DQ S2-4 Discuss some specific reasons why it is important for an organization to proceed with a systems development project even when there is doubt as to the feasibility of the proposed development effort.

DQ S2-5 Exhibit S1.1 (page 18), which outlines the feasibility document, proposes that solutions to the development problem be projected at the conclusion of the systems survey. The outline also suggests that the costs and benefits (economic feasibility) of these solutions be projected. Isn't it premature to know the solutions and their costs and benefits? Explain your answer.

DQ S2-6 Discuss circumstances making a project plan more important than it would be if the circumstances/conditions were not present.

DQ S2-7 One of the goals of systems analysis is to choose and justify one of the alternative design solutions. Would it not be more effective, efficient, and practical for the systems analyst to pass along *all* alternative design solutions to top management (perhaps to the IT steering committee), together with arguments for and against each alternative, and let top management choose one of them? After all, top management has a broad perspective that the systems analyst does not possess. Discuss fully.

DQ S2-8 Discuss the decisions that must be made prior to initiating structured systems analysis. Indicate how the systems survey contributed to the decisions.

DQ S2-9 Discuss the trade-offs of too broad an analysis scope versus too narrow an analysis scope.

DQ S2-10 Indicate whom you would include on a systems analysis project team in each of the following situations, and discuss fully the reasons why you would include each member you suggest.

a. A college's system for tracking students from "cradle to grave" (i.e., from the time that prospective students apply for admission until the time that alumni die and are listed in the "In Memoriam" section of the alumni magazine).

b. A bank's system for *integrating* the various, previously separate affiliations that it has with its customers.

c. A *responsibility accounting/reporting system*, as discussed in Chapter 16 of the accompanying textbook. (*Note:* Discuss only if you have studied Chapter 16 of the accompanying textbook.)

d. A *materials requirements planning (MRP) system*, as discussed in Chapter 15 of the accompanying textbook. (*Note:* Discuss only if you have studied Chapter 15 of the accompanying textbook.)

DQ S2-11 "We can spend too much time studying and documenting the current physical environment." Discuss fully.

DQ S2-12 "In studying and documenting the current physical environment, we usually gather, analyze, and document simultaneously." Discuss and give examples.

DQ S2-13 "If a new information system can't pay for itself, we won't develop it." Discuss fully.

DQ S2-14 Propose ways that the following intangible and/or indirect costs and benefits *might* be measured. Discuss whether they are indirect and/or intangible.

a. Decreased worker productivity.

b. Increased customer support in the form of improved product service and maintenance.

c. Increased customer support in the form of more timely and accurate responses to customer inquiries.

d. Deteriorated vendor relations, as evidenced by more stringent credit terms offered by vendors.

e. Deteriorated vendor relations, as evidenced by longer lead times, poorer quality goods, and more frequent backorder situations.

f. Improved management decision making.

g. Improved competitive advantage.

DQ S2-15 "If the results of the cost/benefit analysis do not agree with those of the effectiveness analysis, there is probably no difference among the alternatives." Discuss fully.

DQ S2-16 What tasks described in this chapter would be done differently if we were to purchase an AIS (i.e., from Chapter S1) versus develop it in-house (i.e., from Chapter S2)?

PROBLEMS

P S2-1 The SELL-IT-ALL Company is a wholesale distributor of office supplies. It sells pencils and pens, paper goods (including computer paper and forms), staplers, calendars, and other items, excluding furniture and other major items such as copy machines that you would expect to find in an office. Sales have been growing at 5 percent per year during the last several years. Mr. Big, the SELL-IT-ALL president, recently attended a national office supplies convention. In conversations during that convention, he discovered that sales for SELL-IT-ALL's competitors have been growing at 15 percent per year. Arriving back home, he did a quick investigation and discovered the following:

- SELL-IT-ALL's customer turnover is significantly higher than the industry average.

- SELL-IT-ALL's vendor turnover is significantly lower than the industry average.

- The new market analysis system was supposed to be ready two years ago but has been delayed for more than one year in systems development.

- A staff position, reporting to the president, for a person to prepare and analyze cash budgets was created two years ago but has never been filled.

Mr. Big has called on you to conduct a systems survey of this situation. You are to assume that a request for systems development has been prepared and approved. The information system at SELL-IT-ALL is much like that depicted in Chapters 10 through 16 of the accompanying textbook.

Make and describe all assumptions that you believe are necessary to solve any of the following:

a. What are the specific goals of *this* systems survey?

b. Indicate specific *quantifiable* benefits and costs that should be examined in assessing the economic feasibility of any solutions that might be proposed. Explain how you would go about quantifying each benefit or cost.

c. Propose and explain three different scopes for the systems analysis. Use a context diagram to describe each scope alternative. *Hint:* What subsystems *might* be involved in an analysis?

P S2-2 Redraw the following organization chart in Figure S2.7 to improve the efficiency, effectiveness, and control. Your corrections should not require adding any personnel. Indicate on the redrawn chart where you have made improvements. Discuss your improvements and any improvements that you thought of but found you could not incorporate.

Figure S2.7 Organization Chart to Accompany Problem S2-2

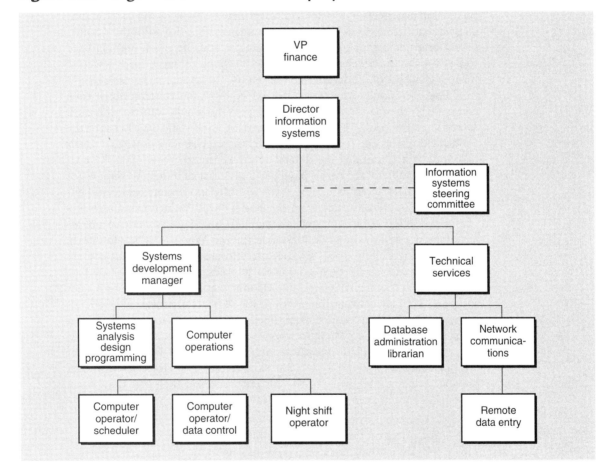

P S2-3 Conduct research of current literature and databases to find reports of systems development project failures. Prepare a report or presentation (as directed by your instructor) describing the failure. Include the elements of feasibility and project risk that may have been miscalculated or mismanaged that led to the project failure.

P S2-4 David's Used Cars is a used car dealership owned and operated by David Steele. Steele has about 200 cars in stock and sells or buys an average of 10 cars per day. Steele buys cars that are trade-ins from new car dealers, repossessions from banks, and cars sold at auctions by municipal towing yards and insurance companies. Steele currently employs two full-time salespeople as well as five full-time mechanics who repair and prepare the cars for resale. Steele rarely, if ever, accepts a car in trade as part of the payment for a car he is selling. Steele uses the following procedures relative to the purchase and sale of used cars.

Steele creates a folder for every car that he purchases. He accumulates information on a car in the folder. The folders are maintained in a filing cabinet alphabetically by car make and model. Each car and corresponding folder is assigned a five-digit sequence number for accurate identification on the lot and in advertisements. Each folder contains a preprinted master sheet. Initially, Steele enters the make, model, and year of the car; the purchase date; the name and address of the owner; the price paid; the odometer reading; the car lot parking space number; and the check number used to pay for the car. Steele and one of the mechanics then prepare a second form, a checklist of 25 descriptive criteria used to evaluate the car's condition. Each criterion is evaluated as poor, fair, good, or excellent. Steele then enters on to the master sheet the selling price he would want for the car if no repairs were made. He also prepares a price sticker and attaches it to the windshield of the car. If a repair is made, the mechanic completes a repair description that contains the details of the repair, the cost, and the estimated retail value of the repair based on a price list of industry averages for various standard repairs. Steele files this with the appropriate folder and enters the cost and retail values on to the master sheet. If the repair affects any of the evaluation criteria, he makes the appropriate adjustment to the affected criteria and to the price sticker on the car. When a car is sold, Steele enters the date, selling price, salesperson, and customer name and address on to the master sheet. Steele approves all sales. All sales are for cash or cashier's check. Steele has a checking account that is used solely for car sales and purchases. He uses another account for all other expenses. He transfers money to the second account from the sales and purchase account. After a car is sold, Steele places the corresponding folder in a drawer in his desk. Every Friday, he calculates the salespeople's commissions based on the selling price recorded in the folder. He pays commissions for sales from the previous Friday to Thursday of the current week. He then files the folders by sequence number in the closed car file.

Steele's system is not without problems. Sometimes Steele forgets to change the prices on the car stickers to reflect repairs that have been made. This error frequently is not discovered until an agreement to sell a car to a customer has been reached. He occasionally files the current Friday's folders for cars sold this week in the closed car file, along with the folders for cars on which the sales commissions already have been paid. As a result, the salespeople do not receive the proper commission for the cars they sold in the most recent week. He also has found that some cars are on the lot for a long time before they are sold. However, Steele has not had the time to look at this problem closely enough to identify all such cars and to get them sold.

In spite of occasional help from his daughter, Steele still spends a lot of time on paperwork. This frustrates him because the information is still frequently inaccurate and processing the paperwork takes time away from managing the business and selling more cars. He believes that the inefficient use of his time is costing him money.

Steele has had no formal business education and has never used a computer. The thought of having to learn about computers scares him. However, he has read about how well computers can simplify manual clerical operations. He has also read that once a computer system has information stored in it, information can be used to generate all kinds of reports that would be useful for analyzing a business and improving cash flow. Steele has hired you to help determine what functions could be automated and how the information would have to be organized to perform those functions.

a. Identify two significant *operational* deficiencies and two significant *information system control* deficiencies. Next to each deficiency, suggest a potential solution. Present your answer in the following form:

Deficiency	**Proposed Solution**
Operational:	
1.	
2.	
Information system control:	
3.	
4.	

Significant means a deficiency that results in one or more *business exposures* (see Exhibit 7.1, page 228).

From the goal columns that would appear in a control matrix, the following definitions apply. *Operational* deficiencies compromise process effectiveness, efficiency of resource use, or security of resources. For example, a redundant process procedure would result in inefficient use of resources. *Information system control* deficiencies undermine the goals of validity, completeness, or accuracy.

b. Suggest some *possible* effects that the installation of a computer-assisted information system might have on (1) the organizational structure of David's Used Cars (job functions, realignment of duties, reporting responsibilities, etc.), and (2) the *behavior* of salespeople, mechanics, customers, or Steele himself.

P S2-5 Review the discussion of the new cash receipts system for Causeway (Figure S2.6 on page 55, Exhibit S2.7 on page 57, and related discussions). Speculate as to the criteria that might be used to select either the direct biller or third-party consolidator method for billing and cash receipts. If your instructor so directs, conduct research to determine how these methods work and the benefits of each to a company such as Causeway.

P S2-6 For each problem described, list and explain the documentation you would recommend for gathering and analyzing related facts. *Note:* It is *not* necessary to simulate the documentation. Confine your answer to a listing and brief explanation (one to two sentences) for each type of documentation that you recommend.

     a. College admissions office is experiencing a decline in applications.

     b. College admissions office is experiencing a decline in the percentage of students coming to the college after being accepted by the college.

     c. Company is experiencing an increase in the size of receivables.

     d. Faculty member has noticed that fewer students are signing up for her classes.

KEY TERMS

systems development

systems development life cycle

quality assurance (QA)

ISO 9000-3

Capability Maturity Model® (SW-CMM®) for Software

systems development methodology

systems development life cycle (SDLC) methodology

deliverables

signoffs

business process reengineering (BPR)

systems survey

feasibility study

preliminary feasibility study

structured systems analysis

logical specification

physical requirements

approved systems analysis document

cost/effectiveness study

cost/benefit study (cost/benefit analysis)

effectiveness study (effectiveness analysis)

direct costs

indirect costs

tangible cost

intangible cost

nonrecurring costs

recurring costs

direct benefits

indirect benefits

tangible benefits

intangible benefits

chapter S3

Learning Objectives

- To enumerate the goals, plans, tasks, and results of systems selection.
- To learn the fundamentals of software specifications and designs.
- To describe the process of choosing computer hardware.
- To recognize how the accountant is involved in systems selection.
- To enumerate the goals, plans, tasks, and results of structured systems design.
- To understand the advantages of structured systems design.
- To appreciate the importance of planning for systems implementations.
- To understand how the accountant is involved in structured systems design.

Systems Selection and Design

Under Joe Hopper's leadership, Hopper Specialty Company had grown into the biggest distributor of industrial hardware in northwest New Mexico. To provide the systems infrastructure needed for future growth, Joe acquired a turnkey[1] inventory management system from NCR. In addition to the NCR hardware and systems software, the system included the Warehouse Manager software from Taylor Management Systems. The system was supposed to track the thousands of items in the Hopper inventory, including prices and balances. However, had Joe thoroughly investigated and tested this system, he would have discovered that:

- Warehouse Manager had not worked anywhere on an NCR computer.
- When two terminals accessed the system at once, both terminals locked up.
- When the locked terminals went back online, information—including prices, item balances, and general ledger data—was altered.
- Sales at the counter were supposed to take fractions of a second. Actual response times were as long as several minutes.

How could Joe have prevented this from happening to his company? Joe needed to conduct a more thorough investigation of the vendors and of existing installations of the proposed system. Also, prior to implementation, the system should have been tested in an environment that resembled the one in which the system was to operate.

---

[1] Recall from Chapter S1 that with a turnkey system the buyer need only "turn the key" to begin operating the system and should need to contact only one vendor to obtain support.

SYNOPSIS

In this chapter, we continue the presentation of the systems development process begun in Chapter S2. We discuss and illustrate the third and fourth steps in systems development: systems selection and structured systems design. In systems selection we assess the software specifications and choose the hardware resources to implement a new or revised system. The hardware selection portion of this task applies to acquired systems (Chapter S1) or in-house developed systems, as discussed in this chapter and Chapter S2. In structured systems design we refine the software specifications for the new or revised business process application and prepare implementation plans. In Appendix S3, we describe *computer-aided software engineering (CASE)*—technology used to automate the systems development process.

CONTROLS

As with earlier chapters in this supplement, one goal of our presentation is to highlight the *controls* that will help us achieve our systems development objectives as we conduct systems selection and design. For example, we describe the hardware testing that may be necessary during the systems selection process.

ENTERPRISE SYSTEMS

E-BUSINESS

We also point out the aspects of these systems development steps that are most affected by the implementation of *enterprise systems* and *e-Business* systems. Our discussion of e-Business includes the use of some *Internet*-based software and hardware resources to implement the new or revised information system.

Recall from earlier discussions that certain systems development tasks are comparable to tasks undertaken in the construction of an industrial park. Systems selection, in which the software design and hardware resources are chosen, is similar to drafting blueprints and choosing contractors for a construction project. Structured systems design, in which the software is designed and the implementation is planned, is similar to finalizing blueprints and other construction-related plans.

INTRODUCTION TO SYSTEMS SELECTION

As you can see in Figure S3.1, systems selection lies *between* structured systems analysis (bubble 2.0) and structured systems design (bubble 4.0). Systems selection uses the new system's *functional requirements* (the logical specification) and *physical requirements* that were developed in the analysis phase to decide what software design and hardware resources will be used to implement the new system. Only after preliminary software design elements and hardware resources are chosen does the detailed design begin.

Systems selection is a set of procedures performed to choose the software specifications and hardware resources for an information system. The *systems selection goals* are to:

CONTROLS

- *Determine what computer software design will implement the logical specification developed in structured systems analysis.* The presumption in this chapter is that we have already decided to develop our own system, rather than purchase an AIS solution from an external vendor. When developing an information system, careful attention must be paid to integrating sound internal controls into the software rather than treating controls as a bolt-on afterthought.

- *Determine what computer hardware will satisfy the physical requirements established in structured systems analysis.* We must evaluate and choose the architecture (e.g., client/server, LAN) and the type, manufacturer, and model of each piece

Figure S3.1 Systems Development Life Cycle

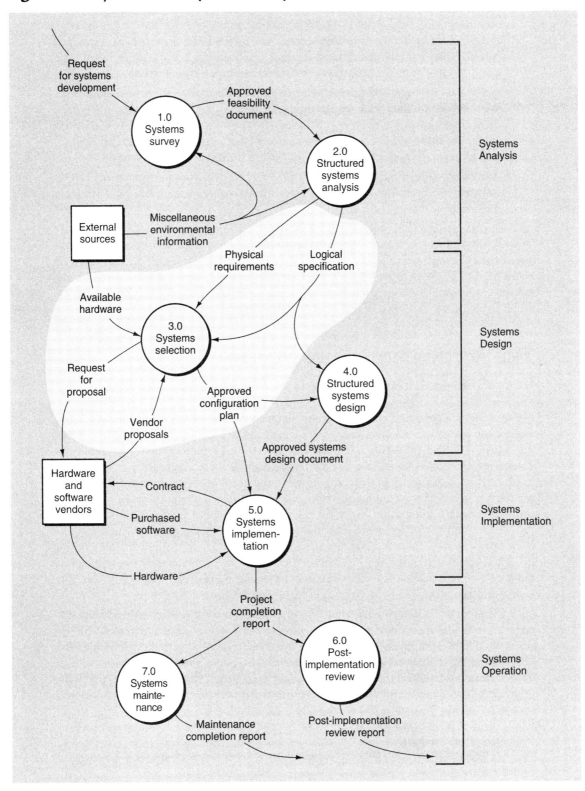

of computer equipment. For instance, we may choose magnetic versus optical disk for file storage, IBM versus Dell for the manufacturer, the appropriate networking configuration, and so on.[2] In making our choice, we should also be cognizant of the implications for the security and control of our information systems. Additionally, to fully understand the cost implications, consideration should be given to environmental controls (i.e., temperature, electrical, etc.).

- *Choose acquisition financing methods that are in the best interest of the organization.* We must decide whether it is better to purchase, rent, or lease the computer equipment. In addition, we must decide if our data center will be completely within our control or if we will use a *service bureau, application service provider* (ASP), *facilities management,* or other *outsourcing* option (as discussed in Chapter S1).

- *Determine appropriate acquisition ancillaries.* We must establish contract terms, software site-licensing arrangements, computer maintenance terms, and software revision procedures and responsibilities.

Before we proceed let us look at the sequence of activities presented in Figure S3.1. Historically, the *logical specification* and the *physical requirements* were developed in the *systems analysis* step *after* the business processes had been documented and accepted or remodeled (e.g., *business process reengineering*). Then, a software solution would be developed in-house. While we present the sequence of the SDLC as "typical," we ask you to be aware of the existence of practical variations in these activities.

THE ACCOUNTANT'S INVOLVEMENT IN SYSTEMS SELECTION

An accountant might become involved in systems selection in the following ways (first introduced in Table S1.2 on page 9). As an analyst, the accountant could be the evaluation team member possessing technical internal control and computer expertise. As a consultant, the accountant could be called on to provide such technical expertise, as well as objectivity. As a user (e.g., staff accountant), the accountant could provide guidance on the tax and financial implications of alternative financing methods. As a user/requester, the staff accountant might be called on to comment on the adequacy of the proposed resource choices. Finally, as an internal auditor, the accountant could serve as a consultant to the evaluation team concerning the controllability and auditability of the proposed resources. Also, the internal auditor might be a member of the evaluation team and be responsible for reviewing and reporting to management about the efficiency and effectiveness of the evaluation team's procedures.

Accounting pronouncements emphasize the importance of the accountant's knowledge in making these software and hardware selections. For example, Statement of Position (SOP) 98-1 requires that most of the costs of software acquired or developed for internal use be capitalized and depreciated over the system's useful life. Prior to SOP 98-1, firms could choose to expense these costs as incurred. Most costs associated with upgrades and enhancements of software are also to be capitalized. Also to be considered

---

[2] An organization's existing hardware might be used to implement a new information system. In this case, the hardware phase of the study would verify that the existing hardware is adequate, given the physical requirements.

is Financial Accounting Standards Board Statement 13, "Lease Capitalization." This statement prescribes the proper accounting for computer equipment leases. In some cases the costs associated with a lease must be expensed, while in other cases it must be capitalized and written off over a number of years.

Additionally, as discussed in Chapter 7 of the accompanying text, Statement on Auditing Standards (SAS) 94 ("The Effect on Information Technology on the Auditor's Consideration of Internal Control in a Financial Statement Audit") offers direction with regard to understanding the impact of IT on internal control and assessing IT-related control risks. SAS 94 also suggests ways in which IT can be used to strengthen internal control and indicates how IT can sometimes weaken control. The guidance offered by SAS 94 will help you to become a valuable member of the systems design team.

THE SYSTEMS SELECTION DELIVERABLE: THE APPROVED CONFIGURATION PLAN

The **approved configuration plan**, the final output of systems selection (see Figure S3.1, page 71), summarizes the choices made in the study. The information in the configuration plan is used in the next phase of systems development, structured systems design, to build the software, acquire the hardware, and develop the implementation plan. The approved configuration plan usually specifies the following items:

- Chosen software configuration and expected performance specifications.
- Chosen hardware type, manufacturer, and model, including expected performance specifications.
- Items to be included in the hardware contracts, such as proposed computer maintenance procedures and proposed procedures by which vendors will provide hardware revisions.
- Results of testing alternative software design and hardware resources.
- Assessment of financing and outsourcing alternatives.

TRIGGERING SYSTEMS SELECTION

The structured systems analysis step (Chapter S2) provides the two key inputs that trigger systems selection:

1. *Logical specification*, which outlines the operations, information, and control requirements of the new system's inputs, outputs, data, and processes.
2. *Physical requirements*, which specify the computer hardware capabilities needed to implement the new system, as well as computer output that is expected from the new system.

As indicated in Chapter S1, a company can decide to purchase an AIS solution from an external vendor, rather than developing an in-house solution. If acquisition is chosen over development, there are alternative ways to purchase an AIS, as discussed in Chapter S1. Similarly, there are alternative ways to acquire needed computer hardware, as discussed next. The hardware issues raised next apply to situations where an AIS is acquired from an external vendor (Chapter S1) or developed internally (Chapters S2 and S3).

HARDWARE ACQUISITION ALTERNATIVES

Before we proceed to the intermediate steps in systems selection, let us spend time examining the various hardware procurement options that an organization must consider. Hardware can be acquired (rented, leased, or purchased) by an organization and managed by the organization's personnel. Alternatively, the hardware can be owned and managed by external entities. Table S3.1 compares these external and internal sources for computer hardware. A review of the table should lead you to conclude that external sources usually provide more capacity and affect the organization's resources less, whereas internal sources can be matched more easily with the organization's needs. We discuss next the major hardware sources.

Table S3.1 Internal Versus External Hardware Sources

Internal	External
Can determine level of control, security, and privacy.	Level of control may vary and be difficult to attain, especially if many companies use the same hardware.
Management and staff must be in-house.	Management and staff are provided.
Capacity limited.	Additional capacity may be available.
Costs are mostly fixed.	Costs are mostly variable.
Tailored to our needs.	Tailoring varies.

Internal Acquisition

Computer hardware can be purchased, rented, or leased from the manufacturer (vendor) or from a leasing company. In such cases, the hardware is acquired, installed in the organization's facilities, and operated by the organization's personnel. As noted in Table S3.1, possession and management by the organization (internal hardware source) is less flexible (because of fixed cost and limited capacity, for example) than is the use of external sources, but it does permit the organization to control and tailor the system.

External Acquisition

An organization preferring not to own or manage its own computer facilities can use three of the hardware alternatives previously described in Chapter S1—a *service bureau*, *outsourcing*, or an *ASP*—to fulfill its hardware needs. A service bureau can provide the services less expensively and in a timelier manner than would be possible with an in-house computer. The main advantage of using a service bureau is that the user organization does not have to operate and maintain the computing resource. If it uses a service bureau, however, the organization must be willing to sacrifice its independence and must compromise scheduling and data security.

Outsourcing has come to encompass many of the external hardware acquisition alternatives that have been available for years. The new twist to these alternatives is the ownership by the outsourcing firm of the user organization's computer facility. In the case of the Kodak–IBM arrangement, for example, IBM purchased Kodak's data centers. Organizations can retain management of their IT while obtaining some application functionality through application service providers (ASPs) in a more flexible and less costly way than through a service bureau.

Facilities management reflects management by a third party of an organization's computer equipment. The equipment is usually owned or leased by the organization, installed on the organization's property, and managed by an external entity that specializes in offering such management services to several clients. The company pays a fee to the facilities management firm and thereby avoids many of the problems associated with managing a computer facility (e.g., hiring, retaining, and supervising computer personnel).

Generally, organizations using facilities management prefer not to deal with the personnel and other operational issues of managing their own data processing department. User organizations must be willing to sacrifice flexibility and control over their IT facility.

Financing Alternatives

Computer hardware can be acquired through purchase, rental, lease, or a combination of these methods. The most popular method of acquiring computer equipment is to *purchase* it from the vendor, paying in full at the time it is received. Purchasing used computer equipment from computer leasing companies, computer users, or the vendor is another favored purchasing method. Purchases can be made with cash but, as with most other capital expenditures, are often financed with a loan.

An organization can *rent* computer equipment from a vendor for a monthly fee. Rental agreements are generally short term—30 to 180 days—and can be canceled by the user organization on short notice. The computer rental alternative is quite expensive, but it does provide flexibility.

An organization can *lease* computer equipment for a monthly fee, which is less than the comparable monthly rental fee. Agreements generally run three to five years and are either *financing* or *operating* leases. Leasing is less costly than rental but is also less flexible, given the longer time commitment required.

In comparing computer purchase, rental, and leasing, we can note the following:

- Rental is the most costly and most flexible alternative.

- In cases of a *temporary* need for computing resources, rentals can be attractive because they require only a short-term commitment and offer the flexibility to meet new demands and utilize the newest computer technology. However, because of their high cost, rentals are impractical for *long-term* needs.

- Financial managers, wanting long-term commitments in order to keep costs down, smooth cash flows, and reduce taxes (through depreciation deductions) prefer financing leases.

- When faced with a dynamic environment, unpredictable rate of growth, and general uncertainty, an organization will prefer leasing or rental over purchase because a user can cancel the commitment with a relatively short notice (in some cases, a cancellation penalty must be paid). This frees the user to acquire different hardware, which might be more up to date or in some way better able to meet the user's needs.

- In comparison to an operating lease, both a financed purchase and a financing lease will cause a greater initial cash outflow (because of the up-front, lump-sum payment required). Furthermore, both will increase debt levels on the balance sheet.[3]

THE INTERMEDIATE STEPS IN SYSTEMS SELECTION

Figure S3.2, a lower-level view of process number 3.0 in Figure S3.1 (page 71), outlines the *systems selection tasks and documents* necessary to achieve the systems selection goals discussed earlier. We will now discuss each task shown in bubbles 3.1, 3.2, 3.3, and 3.4.

Figure S3.2 Systems Selection Tasks and Documents

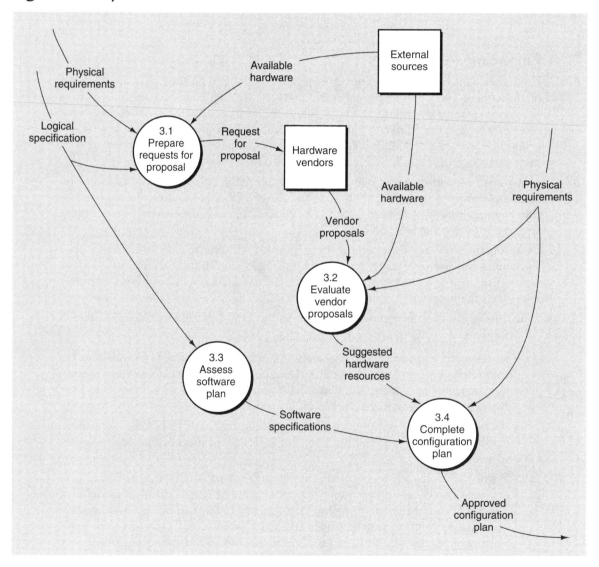

---

[3] See Financial Accounting Standards Board Statement 13, "Lease Capitalization," and any good advanced accounting text for a discussion of financing and operating leases. See also Statement of Position (SOP) 98-1, "Accounting for the Costs of Computer Software Developed or Obtained for Internal Use."

Prepare Requests for Proposal

The first task in Figure S3.2 is to prepare requests for proposal (bubble 3.1). The request for proposal (RFP) topic was covered in Chapter S1 with regard to acquiring an AIS solution from an external vendor. The same procedures should be applied to acquiring hardware solutions from external vendors. Herein, we briefly review such procedures. Recall from Chapter S1 that a *request for proposal (RFP)* is a document sent to vendors that invites submission of plans for providing, in this case, hardware and related services.

Choose Approach to Proposals

Before preparing any requests for proposal, a firm must decide what approach will be taken for soliciting the proposals. An organization can ask one vendor for a proposal, or it can ask many. An organization satisfied with its present vendor might send an RFP to only that vendor. An organization might choose to stay with its present vendor to minimize program conversion costs, to obtain attractive contract clauses (such as discounts or future benefits), and to reduce retraining costs. Also, if an organization has a specialized need that can be met by only one vendor, the organization might send an RFP to only that vendor. Finally, organizations either not possessing the expertise or not wishing to spend the time preparing RFPs and evaluating responses might request a proposal from a single vendor. Unless an organization has a particular reason for limiting its RFPs to a single vendor, however, submission to several vendors is preferred because with multiple proposals an organization has a variety of possibilities from which to choose. In addition, vendor concessions and discounts can be obtained if an organization retains a bargaining position by dealing with several vendors.

The organization can request bids on *specific computer configurations* (e.g., request a bid for Model "XYZ") or to meet general *performance objectives* (e.g., request a bid for a computer system capable of handling the entry of 5,000 business events, such as customer orders, each hour). The former approach leads to a simple evaluation of proposals, but it assumes that the systems analyst preparing the RFP knows what equipment will meet the organization's requirements. The latter approach allows vendors to *propose solutions* to an organization's requirements; the organization may not have anticipated some of these solutions. Choices made from solutions generated entirely within the organization may be suboptimal.

Choose Vendors to Solicit

After deciding how to prepare the requests (i.e., the approach to be used), the organization must then decide to which *specific* vendors the RFPs will be sent. Vendors from whom the organization has previously received proposals or with whom it has previously done business are candidates for receiving proposals. The analysts assigned to conduct systems selection also might research vendor evaluations published in the computer press or in other computer-based or paper-based services. This research is described in Technology Summary S3.1 (page 78).

Complete Requests

Using the information contained in the *logical specification* and/or in the *physical requirements*, the analysts prepare the RFPs and send them to the chosen vendors. Exhibit S1.2 (page 28) from Chapter S1 lists the typical contents of an RFP.

Note that Exhibit S1.2 assumes that the RFP asks for a bid for performance objectives, rather than for a particular computer configuration or product. Some authorities argue that item 4, price and budget constraints, should not be included in the RFP because vendors tend to submit proposals that just meet the budget constraints. These

---

Technology Summary S3.1

Sources of Vendor Information

Analysts can utilize a variety of paper-based, computer-based, and online services to identify and evaluate computer hardware, software, and vendors. The information contained in these services, especially that resulting from independent expert analysis of a vendor and its products or from user surveys, can provide valuable insight into the vendor's quality, financial condition, number of installed systems, and similar information. Some are reports such as those available from Gartner Group, Inc. (http://www.gartner.com). Gartner services include Dataquest Market Intelligence with research and advice in a number of areas including benchmarks, performance measurement, software and hardware products, and vendor selection. Another Gartner service, Datapro, publishes reports in such categories as computer systems and software library, communications library, managing data networks, computers and peripherals, and e-Business and Internet.

Magazines—both printed and online—also provide independent reviews of vendors, hardware, and software. For example ZDNet (http://www.zdnet.com) publishes reviews in their online magazine *eWEEK* and in magazines that are both printed and published online, such as *PC Magazine* and *Computer Shopper*.

In addition to these independent sources of information about software, hardware, and vendors, the Internet provides a wealth of information directly from the vendors. For example, in a quick tour of the Web (November 2000), sites were found for Symantec (network security, virus protection, etc.—http://www.smallbiz.symantec.com), IBM (http://www.ibm.com), Microsoft (http://www.microsoft.com), SAP (http://www.sap.com), J.D. Edwards (http://www.peoplesoft.com), and Gateway (http://www.gateway.com). Through these sites, news was obtained about upcoming products, lists of existing products, customer support, technical support, software purchases, and software fixes and upgrades.

Finally, in addition to traditional software vendors, you can connect via virtual meeting places on the Internet, such as those operated by SourceXchange.com (http://www.SourceXchange.com), Cosource.com (http://www.Cosource.com), and Open-Avenue Inc. (http://www.openavenue.com), with open-source programmers. These programmers may be able to meet your software needs in less time and for less money than would be the case through other means. They build applications using existing open-source components rather than develop them from scratch or by using commercial software. Once developed, however, the application is made available to others via the open-source software network. Consequently, open-source programming should not be used for business-critical systems or those that provide a competitive advantage.

Source: Dominique Deckmyn, "Open-Source Projects Get Done Cheaply," *Computerworld* (April 24, 2000): 44.

---

authorities believe that vendors will inflate their proposals to get the price up to the user's expected price or will propose less hardware than is required in order to keep the proposal under the RFP's budget limit.

The section on projected growth requirements is important relative to the RFP. The better an organization accurately projects the long-term requirements for a new system and obtains hardware that can satisfy that long-term demand, the longer it will be before the system needs to be revised and new hardware obtained.

Evaluate Vendor Proposals

The second task shown on Figure S3.2 is to evaluate vendor proposals (bubble 3.2). Using the vendor responses to the RFP and the physical requirements, the analysts must decide which, if any, proposal best meets the organization's needs. The process of evaluating the vendor proposals includes three steps:

1. Validate vendor proposals.
2. Consider other data and criteria.
3. Suggest resources.

Many organizations assign a team to evaluate the proposals. The team could consist of personnel with IT technical expertise, business process owners, system users, external consultants, lawyers, and accountants. The evaluation team completes these three steps to suggest the hardware and services that best meet the organization's requirements.

The vendor proposals might involve a presentation made by the vendor. This is an example of an external presentation, in which someone from outside the organization (the vendor in this case) makes a presentation of information (the proposal) to members of the organization.

Validate Vendor Proposals

The first evaluation step is to **validate** the vendor proposal to assess whether the system hardware does what the organization requires. Validation consists of two intermediate steps: first-level effectiveness analysis and system testing. To determine whether a system meets the requirements of the RFP, the evaluation team can study a proposed system's specifications and performance.

Specifications are straightforward descriptions of the hardware. For example, the server's storage space or a printer's speed can be examined to determine whether the hardware has sufficient capacity and speed to perform as required. Other specifications include items such as:

- The compatibility of the hardware with other hardware, communication technologies, and operating systems.
- Memory size and potential expandability.
- Maximum storage size and potential expandability.
- Processor speed and potential upgrade.

Performance features can be determined only through testing, measurement, or evaluation and often include items such as:

- Vendor support services, such as training, maintenance, and telephone (or online) help, provided after the hardware is installed. Note that the existence of these support services would be a specification while their effectiveness would be a performance issue.
- Quality of documentation.
- Reliability.
- The scalability of the system. The number of event transactions that must be processed over time often experiences rapid growth spurts. Scalability is the ability of the system to be quickly adapted to meet rapid event transaction processing growth.

One commonly used method for measuring system performance involves measuring the system's **throughput**, which reflects the quantity of work performed in a period of time. For instance, the number of invoices that a system processes in one hour is a measure of throughput. Other performance measures, such as ease of use, are more subjective and may be more difficult to determine.

CONTROLS

E-BUSINESS

If the decision is made to utilize the services of an ASP to deliver hardware and communications capabilities, care must be taken to ensure that the ASP vendor is reliable, because the ultimate fate of your organization lies in the ASP's hands. Accordingly, there are a host of issues to address. Some of the more salient issues are summarized in Technology Excerpt S3.1. A word of caution—be very careful before turning your entire computer processing capacity over to an ASP. While there are many benefits to be realized, the potential risks are high. In particular, you will have less control over processing times and configuration specifications. If you are engaged in e-Business, where your systems are inexorably linked to your trading partners' systems, be especially careful when using the ASP model as a hiccup in your ASP's systems can ripple throughout your entire value chain.

In summary, an evaluation team can measure system specifications or performance. A variety of system or output factors can be measured under a variety of conditions. Either actual or simulated inputs and an actual or a simulated system can be used in these studies as will be described later in this section. Notice that during validation we are not *comparing* vendor proposals; rather, we are determining which proposals can meet our requirements.

First-Level Effectiveness Analysis.   RFPs often distinguish mandatory and desirable system characteristics. As a first step in the validation process, many proposals can be rejected because they fail to meet mandatory effectiveness requirements. Table S3.2 depicts a first-level analysis of proposals and identifies those that do not meet minimum conditions. Notice that the criteria used—only a sample is presented here—represent specifications, not performance aspects, of the system. In first-level effectiveness analysis, we have not yet *tested* the system and can evaluate the system only on the basis of the system's parameters, not the system's performance. Still, even these specifications might not hold up in a test. For example, hardware compatibility may be specified but may not work in certain configurations.

In Table S3.2, vendor B would be rejected for not meeting imperative conditions 1, 3, 4, and 5. This table is for illustration only—it is unlikely that a vendor would respond

---

T e c h n o l o g y   E x c e r p t   S 3 . 1

Issues to Consider When Selecting an ASP

- Information obtained directly from present users of the ASP about the ASP's technical and service capabilities.
- Level of systems availability. How is this measured? Do availability guarantees extend to services employed by the ASP (i.e., secondary ASPs)? What are the penalties for failure to meet targets?
- Provisions for security, data backup, and disaster recovery.
- Capabilities and certifications of technical support and operations person-

nel. What is the staffing at the hosting site? When are they there? Is technical support provided directly or by a third party?
- How much can the hardware be tailored?
- What is covered by the cost?
- The ASP's partners, including their hardware vendors and ASPs from whom they obtain services.

Sources: Excerpted from Gary Anthes, "Avoiding ASP Angst," *Computerworld* (October 16, 2000): 80–81; "Seven Issues to Consider When Using an ASP," Viking Software Solutions (http://www.vikingsoft.com) (November 27, 2000).

Table S3.2 First-Level Hardware Vendor Effectiveness Analysis*

	Vendors		
Criteria	A	B	C
1. Includes five-year all-inclusive warranty	Y	N	Y
2. Hardware is compatible with existing Web servers	Y	Y	Y
3. Processor upgrade is possible	Y	N	Y
4. Utilizes client/server architecture	Y	N	Y
5. Compatible with next larger computer model	Y	N	Y
6. Can be delivered on time	Y	Y	Y

* Y = Proposed system possesses the characteristic.
  N = Proposed system does not possess the characteristic.

to an RFP with a proposal that does not meet four of six minimum requirements. Because lack of a single mandatory requirement can eliminate a vendor proposal from consideration, an organization should judiciously assign mandatory status to a system's requirements. Note that the criteria in Table S3.2 are not necessarily mandatory characteristics in all situations.

Test the System. After completing the first-level effectiveness analysis, the evaluation team tests[4] the remaining systems (i.e., those that satisfy mandatory requirements) to determine the accuracy of the vendors' specifications and how well the equipment will work for the organization. In first-level effectiveness analysis, we determine what a system *is*; in testing, we determine what that system *can do*.

An evaluation team can test a system by:

- Varying input (workload) parameters, such as quantity, timing, and type of input.
- Varying system characteristics (parameters), such as quantity and size of data storage devices.
- Varying the factors being measured, such as CPU cycle time (a system parameter) or execution time (a performance measure).
- Testing an actual workload, such as a weekly payroll, or testing a workload model that is representative of the workload.
- Testing the actual system or a model of the system.

Organizations often use benchmarks to test a computer system during hardware studies. A **benchmark** is a *representative* user workload, processed on each vendor's proposed system configuration, to obtain comparative *throughput* measures. By representative, we mean that the test must include all applications that will share the processing capacity. In this way, the test will determine the impact of the applications on each other. In vendor proposal validation, the benchmark is used to determine the ability of the proposed configuration to meet the user's requirements. Later in the evaluation, the

---

[4] Often, vendors will propose a system that does not actually exist *yet*. In such cases, we cannot test an actual system; our only option is to *simulate* the proposed system, as discussed later in this section.

benchmarks may be compared to suggest which proposal should be accepted. Benchmarking, a relatively costly procedure, may be deferred until that later phase of the evaluation and used only for comparing, rather than validating, proposals.

For example, we might have a benchmark for data storage capacity and speed. To test the benchmark, we would load data on a vendor's machine and then run a job that manipulates that data in some way. This test would tell us if a single vendor's machine will meet our performance requirements. Then, we would perform the same test, using the same data and the same job, on several vendor's machines to see which machine works best for this test.

Consider Other Data and Criteria

Rather than estimate vendor and system performance internally, the evaluation team can interview users of the vendors' products and visit those sites to witness the system in action. Quite often, vendor presentations are made at the site of an existing user. **External interviews**—interviews conducted with personnel outside the organization—can provide valuable insights into vendor performance. Where appropriate, questionnaires can be used to gather information from users. The following information might be collected from users:

- Were there delays in obtaining the hardware?
- Did the system have bugs?
- How responsive is the vendor to requests for service?
- Was the training the vendor provided adequate?

As mentioned in Technology Summary S3.1 (page 78), there are several services that publish technical reviews, user surveys, and expert commentary on computer systems and a variety of related topics. The reviews and user surveys can be helpful when evaluating proposals.

A cost/benefit analysis, similar to those discussed in Chapters S1 and S2, is often used to determine the economic viability of the remaining vendor proposals. Quantifiable costs and benefits are summarized to determine whether vendor proposals can be justified economically. Ranking of vendor proposals using the economic criteria is useful in the next step in systems selection, in which the evaluation team suggests which vendor proposal to choose.

Suggest Resources

At this point, the study team must recommend one vendor proposal. Management then chooses the hardware resources. To recommend one vendor, the evaluation team must compare the proposals that have not been eliminated. The evaluation team might list the relevant criteria and indicate the performance of each vendor on each criterion. Table S3.3 depicts such an analysis. The criteria—as with Table S3.2, only a sample has been presented here—would be those indicated in the *logical specification* and *physical requirements* as well as any others the evaluation team considers important. The evaluation team uses the performance measures gathered during system testing and when other data and criteria were considered. For example, the results of the benchmark test could be summarized in this analysis and used to compare performance.

The analysis from Table S3.3 might not clearly indicate a superior vendor. It is normally advisable and necessary to perform an analysis that assigns scores to each vendor on each relevant criterion. In addition to scoring each, the evaluation team ranks the importance of each criterion by assigning it a weight. Of course, the comparison is only as

Table S3.3 Detailed Vendor Comparison

Criteria	Vendors		
	A	B	C
Documentation quality	good	good	poor
Cost of typical configuration	$53,630	$29,900	$59,300
Monthly maintenance of typical configuration	$422	$515	$448
Maximum number of workstations	8	32	32
Benchmark results:			
Number of invoices/minute	2	4	6
Query response time (seconds)	1	1.5	2.0

valid as the weights and scoring values used. Also, if the results of this analysis agree with the previous evaluations and the intuition of the evaluation team, then the team receives a certain amount of comfort from this analysis. Finally, using this type of weighted scoring system facilitates communication of the team's recommendations to the *IT steering committee* and the user, and thus helps gain support for that recommendation.

Assess Software Plan

The next task in the systems selection step is to assess software plans (see Figure S3.2, bubble 3.3, page 76). This task begins by using the logical specifications from the systems analysis phase (Chapter S2). Recall that logical specifications describe how the new or revised system is expected to function. For instance, if an organization is changing its business process from cash only sales to cash and credit card sales, the new system would be expected to handle credit card authorizations and payments in addition to cash. Thus, the logical specifications would indicate such additional cash receipts functionality.

Assessing software plans results in software specifications, which are used in structured systems design (see Figure S3.1, bubble 4.0, page 71). The basic procedures involved are designing databases, designing forms and reports, and designing interfaces and conversions.

Designing Databases

The design of databases was discussed in Chapter 6 of the accompanying text. Hence, the main issues will be briefly covered here. When designing the database for the new or revised system, you must make sure that you have accounted for all entity types (resources, events, and agents) involved in the system. The illustration shown in Figure S3.3 (page 84) is a handy way to visualize entity types that are typically affected and must be considered when developing an information system.

With most any business process event, economic resources are forfeited (outflow) and gained (inflow). For instance, when a retail store sells a pair of shoes in exchange for U.S. dollars, the store gives up the shoes and receives the money. In this example, the outflow economic event is the shoe sale and the inflow event is the cash receipt. Notice the duality between outflow and inflow events; that is, a resource is given and received.

Figure S3.3 Resources, Events, and Agents

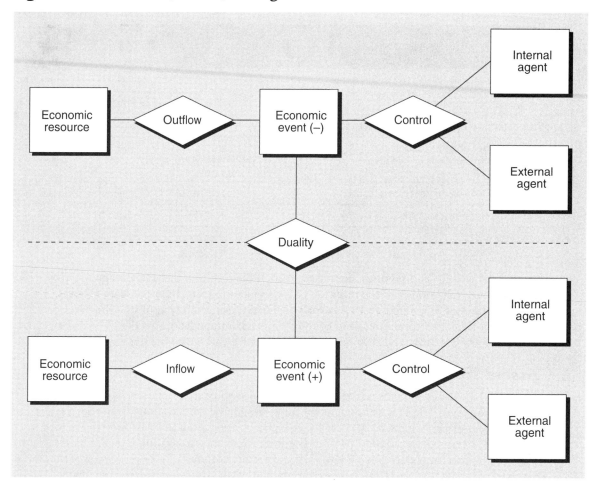

Source: Adapted from C. L. Dunn and W. E. McCarthy, "The REA Accounting Model: Intellectual Heritage and Prospects for Progress," *Journal of Information Systems* 11 (1) (Spring, 1997): 31–51.

Associated with each economic event are one or more agents. Some agents are internal to the organization and others are external. Following our simple example, the internal agent for the sale is a salesperson and the external agent is the customer. Regarding the inflow event, the internal agent is a cashier and the external agent, again, is the customer. This is a very logical and comprehensive way to envision the entity types involved in the new or modified system under development. Once all resources, events, and agents are identified, the systems designer can begin to design the database tables, relationships, and attributes, as discussed in Chapter 6 of the text.

Designing Forms and Reports

During the systems analysis phase of the SDLC (Chapter S2), we briefly discussed the importance of identifying user screens and reports, also known as system outputs. At this point, the systems designers need to further develop such outputs—specifications that will be finalized in the next chapter (Chapter S4). Basically, at this point in the SDLC, we need to know what the purpose of the output is, who will use the output, when the output will be required, where the output will appear, and how many users need access to the output. Screen and print output should include meaningful titles, relevant information, aesthetically appealing layout, and in the case of computer screens, easy navigation.

Also, screen outputs in particular might need to draw the users' attention to certain screen areas or elements. For instance, consider a salesperson who is attempting to process a credit card sales transaction. If the customer's card cannot be accepted (for whatever reason), the screen might blink Credit Card Not Authorized. In another instance, if a salesperson is taking a telephone order but the inventory item that the customer wants is not in the warehouse, the screen might flash in a vivid color Not in Stock. Various methods of attracting attention on computer screens are underlines, font types and sizes, color differences, blinking and flashing messages, sounds, motion, boxes, and intensity differences. Be cautious, however, to use such attention-grabbing features very sparingly, because too many on one screen will overwhelm the user and result in confusion.

Additionally, it is important that screen and print outputs are user-friendly. While this might seem obvious, many software programs are unnecessarily difficult for users, because the systems were designed by technical people who did not consult with users. It is imperative that systems designers involve users in assessing the usability of system outputs. Some of the main usability features are consistency (e.g., formatting, titles, terms, and navigation), satisfactory response times, efficient layouts to facilitate quick and accurate data input, and flexible and adaptable interface features so that each user can tailor the look and feel of the system to meet his cognitive style. How might the systems designer measure usability? Metrics such as learning time, retention time, response time, and error rates can help designers to assess and improve usability of system outputs. Chapter S4 will continue to refine screens and reports.

Designing Interfaces and Conversions

The next consideration in assessing software plans is the preliminary design of *interfaces* (how the new or revised IS will talk with existing systems) and *conversions* (how to reformat data from the old system to the new system). If the new IS totally replaces all other systems in the organization, then there might be no need to design interfaces. However, with most systems development projects, the new system is a subsystem of the *enterprise system*. Also, there may be no need to convert data from the old to the new format if the new system will utilize the existing data definitions. However, in many cases, there is a need to convert data, because the old format is inconsistent with the new format. Recognize that detailed plans and execution of conversions will take place during systems implementation; however, at this point in the SDLC, the developers should begin thinking about and planning for data conversions.

ENTERPRISE SYSTEMS

Regarding interfaces, assume for a moment that the systems development objective is to build a new payroll system. Linked to the payroll system are employee benefits and human resources information systems—both components of the human resources management process described in Chapter 14 of the accompanying text. The benefits system is outsourced to an external benefit provider and the human resources system was purchased from an external vendor. The new payroll system, while developed in-house, must pass and receive data to and from the benefits and HR systems in the format each system expects. While there are many ways to handle these situations depending on the complexities involved, Figure S3.4 (page 86) illustrates one possibility.

The over-simplified example shown in Figure S3.4 depicts three formats for company number (x), division number (y), and unique ID number (z). The employee benefits

ENTERPRISE SYSTEMS

Figure S3.4 Interfaces among Payroll, Benefits, and Human Resources Systems

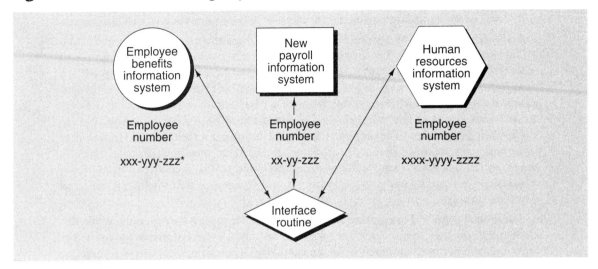

* x = company, y = division, and z = unique employee ID number.

system needs these numbers in sets of three digits each, the human resources system uses sets of four digits each, and the new payroll system is designed for two digits each for company and division numbers and three digits for the unique employee ID. The interface routine will translate these formats among the three related information systems as necessary. Oftentimes, *enterprise systems* are threaded with many interface routines, particularly if the subsystems of the enterprise system reflect a combination of external and internal systems. Even internally developed systems might need interface routines in order to communicate, especially if the systems were developed at different times by different designers.

Conversion routines are needed when the new system is brought online. While interfaces operate continuously, conversions reflect one-time-use routines that are focused on reformatting data from old to new formats. Referring once again to the example shown in Figure S3.4, say that the old payroll system used the format x-y-zzz for employee number. When converting data from the old to new systems, the conversion routine would have to take the old company number, x, and convert it to xx, probably by adding 0 as the first digit. The same routine would take place for the division number and unique ID number. Once this is accomplished, the new system is off and running.

Complete Configuration Plan

To complete the *configuration plan* (see Figure S3.2, bubble 3.4, page 76), the evaluation team must:

1. Complete the software plan.
2. Complete the hardware plan.
3. Prepare the configuration plan.
4. Obtain approvals.

As with many of the steps in systems development, these processes are not necessarily sequential, and are often iterative.

Using the *logical specification* as a guide, the evaluation team must complete the software plan. The **software plan** documents how the logical specification will be implemented. Although the hardware study may precede or be conducted simultaneously with the software study, the software plan must be completed before the hardware plan, because hardware selections may be determined by software requirements.

Using the *physical requirements* and software plan as a guide, the analysts must complete the hardware plan. The **hardware plan** summarizes how the recommended vendor proposal will fulfill the physical requirements specified in structured systems analysis.

The configuration plan should document the results of any software and hardware tests and evaluations. This documentation will be used to prepare the contract and, after the system is implemented, to assess the quality of the evaluation team's efforts and the quality of the selected software specifications and acquired hardware. In addition to the software and hardware plans, the configuration plan contains the evaluation team's assessment of the financing alternatives and recommendations for acquisition ancillaries, such as maintenance procedures and software and hardware revisions.

Once the configuration plan is completed, it must be approved by the information systems steering committee, IT management, the internal auditor, the controller, legal counsel, and other appropriate management personnel. Once approved, the configuration plan is used in the next step in systems development—structured systems design.

INTRODUCTION TO SYSTEMS DESIGN

Studies have shown that systems developed using structured systems design techniques are less costly over the *life* of the system because maintenance of the system is less expensive. Also, structured systems design avoids design errors that further increase the cost of the system. Implementation planning, conducted during structured systems design and introduced in this section, increases the probability of a smooth transition to the new information system.

Definition and Goals

Figure S3.5 (page 88) shows that structured systems design is the fourth major step in the development of an information system (bubble 4.0). Examine this figure to see the position that structured systems design holds in the SDLC.

Structured systems design is a set of procedures performed to convert the logical specification into a design that can be implemented on the organization's computer system. Concurrent with specification of the system's design, *plans* are developed for testing and implementing the new system and for training personnel. Portions of the user manual are also developed at this time.

Let us return to our earlier analogy between systems development and the construction of an industrial park. Converting the information system's logical specification into detailed design specifications is similar to finalizing the construction blueprints. The models developed earlier in the construction project are not detailed enough to allow the actual construction to begin; final blueprints provide that detail. Also, planning must be undertaken to determine the construction schedule for the buildings. Pre-construction planning is analogous to the computer system implementation planning done at this juncture in the SDLC. For example, the development team must plan how much of the system to implement and when.

Figure S3.5 Systems Development Life Cycle

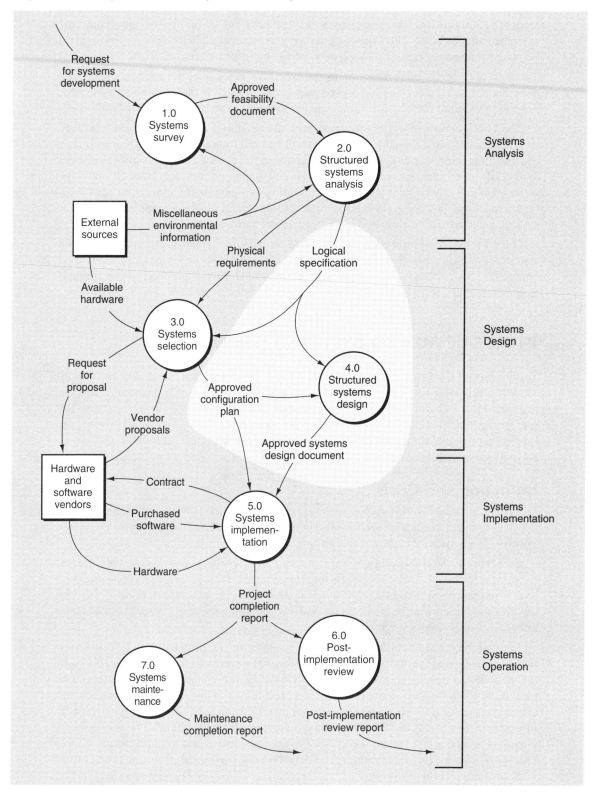

The structured systems design goals are as follows:

- *Convert the structured specification into a reliable, maintainable design.* This is similar to the process of converting the building model into a final blueprint.
- *Develop a plan and budget that will ensure an orderly and controlled implementation of the new system.* Procedures must be devised to get the hardware in place, the programming completed, the training conducted, and the new system operating.
- *Develop an implementation test plan that ensures that the system is reliable, complete, and accurate.* A plan must be developed to test the system to ensure that it does what the user wants it to do.
- *Develop a user manual that facilitates efficient and effective use of the new system by operations and management personnel.* These personnel must know how to use the new system effectively, and the information processing staff must know how to operate the system.
- *Develop a program that ensures that users and support personnel are adequately trained.*

Systems Design Tasks

Figure S3.6 (page 90), a lower-level view of process 4.0 in Figure S3.5, outlines the *structured systems design tasks and documents* necessary to achieve the systems design goals. After describing the accountants' involvement in systems design, we will discuss each element in the figure. We start with the output deliverable (the approved systems design document), then the inputs that trigger systems design, and finally the intermediate steps (bubbles 4.1 through 4.6).[5]

THE ACCOUNTANT'S INVOLVEMENT IN SYSTEMS DESIGN

An accountant might participate in structured systems design in the following ways (first introduced in Table S1.2 on page 9). As an analyst, the accountant could be a member of the design team who is responsible for preparing the software specifications, implementation plans, or testing plans. As a consultant, the accountant could be called on for her technical expertise in the design process. As a user (e.g., staff accountant), he can help develop implementation plans, test plans, training plans, and the user manual. Also, the accountant can review the software specifications for correspondence with the logical requirements. Finally, as an internal auditor, the accountant can review the design process to determine its efficiency and effectiveness and its conformity with the organization's systems development standards. As well, internal auditors can test the effectiveness of embedded internal controls.

THE SYSTEMS DESIGN DELIVERABLE: THE APPROVED SYSTEMS DESIGN DOCUMENT

The **approved systems design document**, the final deliverable of structured systems design (see Figure S3.5), documents the systems design; summarizes the implementation,

---

[5] Although structured systems design should relate only to bubble 4.0 in Figure S3.5, we use the terms *structured systems design* and *systems design* interchangeably.

Figure S3.6 Structured Systems Design Tasks and Documents

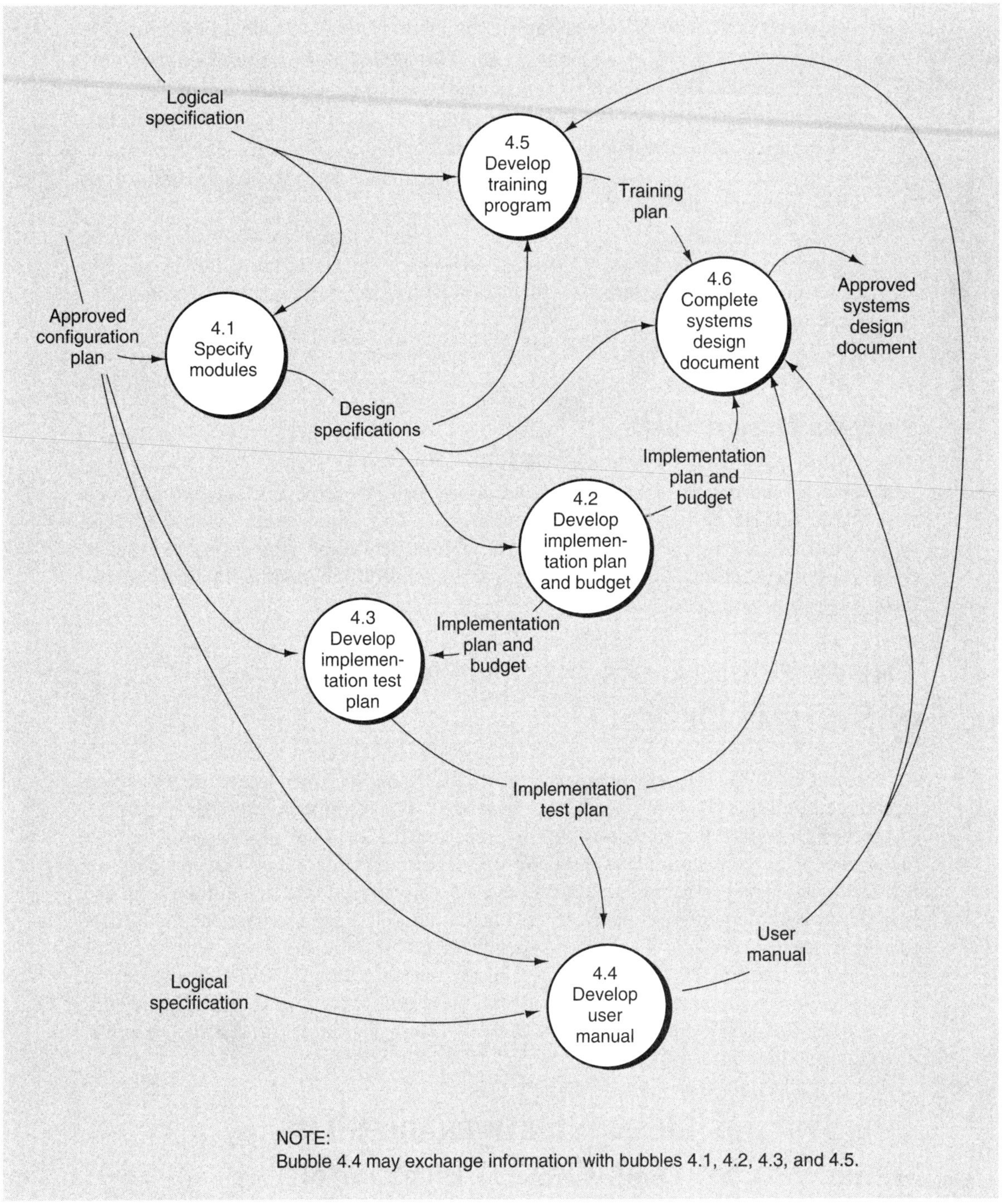

NOTE:
Bubble 4.4 may exchange information with bubbles 4.1, 4.2, 4.3, and 4.5.

training, and test plans; and contains the portions of the user manual that have been developed through that point. The design document is used by the:

• Programmers to write the computer programs and program interfaces.

- Personnel department to develop and conduct training and education programs.
- Information systems personnel to test and implement the system.

Approved systems design document usually specifies the following items:

- *Design specifications.* Detailed plans are included for executing the system's logical processes, including a detailed design for each program; design diagrams (structure charts); description of logical processes; and descriptions of inputs, outputs, database tables, and program interfaces. Also, the specifications describe how each program is grouped into subsystems and systems.
- *Implementation plan and budget.* A description of the steps required to implement the new system is provided. A schedule of resources required for the implementation is included.
- *Implementation test plan.* A description of the tests required to validate the system prior to its operation is provided.
- *User manual.* Preliminary portions of the manual are included that provide instructions on how to use the new system.
- *Training plan.* A description of the training program required for system users and the personnel who will operate the system is provided.

TRIGGERING SYSTEMS DESIGN

Refer again to Figure S3.5 (page 88) and note that structured systems design follows structured systems analysis *and* systems selection and has as its two major inputs:

1. The logical specification.

2. The approved configuration plan.

The approved configuration plan, developed in systems selection, determines the nature and extent of the systems design tasks. For example, the hardware specifications and tests conducted to select a configuration suggest some implementation tests. The logical specification dictates the logic required in the new design.

THE INTERMEDIATE STEPS IN SYSTEMS DESIGN

Specify Modules

The specification of modules is one of the features unique to *structured* systems development. The main tool of the structured design process is the structure chart. The **structure chart** is a graphic tool for depicting the partitioning of a system into modules, the hierarchy and organization of these modules, and the communication interfaces between the modules.[6]

The structure chart's overall appearance is similar to that of an organization chart. Each box on a structure chart is a **module**. These structure chart modules become computer program modules of 30 to 60 lines of computer program code (one-half to one page of code). During structured systems design, related activities are grouped together

---

[6] J. A. Hoffer, J. F. George, and J. S. Valacich, *Modern Systems Analysis and Design*, 3rd ed. (Upper Saddle River, NJ: Prentice Hall, 2002): 503–510.

within a module. This grouping of activities leads to a more maintainable system because changes to one function of a system lead to changes in a minimum of modules.

Develop Implementation Plan and Budget

Systems designers possess valuable insights into how a system should be implemented. During the design phase, these insights are documented in an implementation plan. As the implementation plan evolves, the resources required to implement the new system are summarized into an implementation budget. The project team develops the implementation plan and budget during this phase so that resources can be allocated and the many implementation tasks scheduled before the implementation begins.

The structure chart, developed by the systems designer, dictates which modules should be programmed and installed first, and this sequence becomes part of the plan. The systems designer uses the expected size and complexity of the computer programs to prepare a schedule and budget for the programmers required to write the program code.

Develop Implementation Test Plan

Each system module, and *any combinations thereof*, must be tested prior to implementation. Again, systems designers have valuable insights into how a system should be tested. As we saw in the discussion of structure charts, the inputs and outputs for each module (and module combination) are specified in the design phase. This allows the designers to specify test inputs and expected outputs as well as provide a recommendation for the order in which the system's pieces should be tested.

Develop User Manual

Because the designer knows how the system and each program will operate, how each input should be prepared, and how each output is used, preparation of the user manual can begin in the design phase. At this point in the SDLC, the manual is used to *begin* briefing and training users.

Bubble 4.4 in Figure S3.6 (page 90)—Develop user manual—interacts with several other implementation plans (i.e., bubbles 4.1, 4.2, 4.3, and 4.5), implying that user manual development proceeds concurrently with many other design activities. For example, user procedures developed in bubble 4.4 usually depend on computer system procedures developed in bubble 4.1. Conversely, some system functions specified in bubble 4.1 can depend on user procedures developed in bubble 4.4. As a final example, development team members must know about user procedures (bubble 4.4) so that they can design tests of those procedures (bubble 4.3).

Develop Training Program

User training should begin before the system is implemented and, therefore, must be planned during the design phase. Deciding when to conduct training is tricky. While training must be conducted before implementation, it cannot be too much before or the trainees will forget what they learned. Also, the training materials, user manuals, and system used for training must be consistent with the system that will actually be implemented and used by the trainees.

Complete Systems Design Document

The *approved systems design document* has three main components: (1) the systems design (*structure charts* and descriptions of logical processes); (2) the implementation, testing, and training plans; and (3) the user manual. The design project leader assembles these components and obtains the required user approvals (to ensure the adequacy of the design and plans) and management approvals (to signify concurrence with the design, training, and implementation process). In addition, IS management furnishes a supervisory/technical approval of the adequacy of the software specifications, and auditors ensure adequacy of the controls and the design process (including implementation planning).

SUMMARY

Systems selection is a process that is central to the success of systems development. Recall that the first objective of systems development is to develop information systems that satisfy an organization's informational and operational needs. For this reason, one key to the success of systems development is to ensure that our systems selection criteria are based on the user requirements (i.e., the logical specifications and physical requirements) developed during the systems analysis phase of systems development.

Another key to systems development success is the full evaluation of hardware resources. As the quantity of resources has proliferated, it has become more difficult to identify and adequately evaluate all available resources. On the other hand, the Internet has made available to us large quantities of up-to-date, independent information to assist in the selection process. **E-BUSINESS**

Finally, as noted in the systems design section of this chapter, the success of systems development projects may be found in the details. It may be such things as user manuals, training, and implementation schedules and plans that determine the success of the new or modified system.

APPENDIX S3

Computer-Aided Software Engineering (CASE)

Computer-aided software engineering (CASE) can improve the efficiency *and* effectiveness of systems development. Technology Summary S3.2 describes how CASE is used.

With the background in information systems, computers, and structured systems analysis and design that you have developed in this course, you are well positioned to participate in the CASE-based development and audit of information systems. Internal auditors could become involved in the use of CASE in the following ways:

- Review the systems development methodology utilized with CASE to determine that it is in compliance with corporate and industry standards. For example, you might determine the adequacy of systems documentation.
- Perform an audit of the first application built with CASE to determine the adequacy of the development process and the quality of the new system.

Technology Summary S3.2

Computer-Aided Software Engineering

Computer-aided software engineering (CASE) is the application of computer-based technology to automate the development of information systems. CASE also has been described as the combination of structured development methodologies—such as the approach used in this supplement—and computer-based CASE *tools*. CASE has been used to support:

- Corporate planning and the creation of the business model—the enterprise model. This is often called *upper CASE*, or *front-end CASE*.
- Systems analysis and design. This is often called *middle CASE*. It connects *front-end CASE* with *back-end CASE* and leads to systems specifications such as those described in Chapters S1 and S2.
- Programming and implementation. This is often called *lower CASE* or *back-end CASE* and includes the creation of program structure charts, the generation of program code, and the creation of user documentation. These topics are discussed in this and the next chapter in this supplement.

There are many reasons for using CASE:

- Systems are developed and implemented more quickly. The automatic generation of 60 to 80 percent of program code can by itself shorten the development process. The reduction of the programming time permits systems developers to spend more time on the analysis phase—without lengthening the development process.
- The mundane task of preparing and maintaining documentation is facilitated.
- Development standards can be enforced and errors checked through use of the CASE software. This is more efficient and consistent than manual processes.

- Data, once captured, are shared among members of the development team and passed along to succeeding phases of the development process. This process is more efficient than creating documentation several times, and it leads to more consistent and complete systems.
- Systems development is an iterative process in which the system's requirements and design are gradually refined. With CASE, it is easier to make these changes.
- The standardized, automated documentation makes it easier to maintain the system.

CASE systems contain the following features:

- A central repository for data and documentation that links diagrams and data dictionary entries. (For example, the levels of DFDs would be linked together and connected to the definitions of the data flows and data stores contained on the DFDs. These, in turn, would be linked to descriptions of the screens and documents associated with the inputs and outputs.)
- Prototyping for screens, reports, and other outputs.
- Project management.
- Automated diagramming for documentation, such as DFDs.
- DFD integrity checking (e.g., balancing).
- Sharing of design specifications (e.g., data dictionary entries for process logic, database, etc.) among systems development team members.
- Automatic program code generation.

REVIEW QUESTIONS

RQ S3-1 What is systems selection?

RQ S3-2 What are the systems selection goals?

RQ S3-3 How might an accountant participate in systems selection?

RQ S3-4 What are the primary inputs to the hardware study?

RQ S3-5 What does the approved configuration plan specify? What does the software plan specify? What does the hardware plan specify?

RQ S3-6 What are the reasons for using external and internal sources of hardware?

RQ S3-7 What are the relative advantages of renting, leasing, and purchasing computer hardware?

RQ S3-8 What are the factors an organization must consider in structuring the RFP and deciding to whom the RFP will be sent?

RQ S3-9 What is the difference between a specification and a performance measure?

RQ S3-10 What is the difference between benchmark testing and simulation as used in systems selection?

RQ S3-11 What must you consider when designing a database?

RQ S3-12 What must you consider when designing computer outputs?

RQ S3-13 What are the differences between interface and conversion routines?

RQ S3-14 What is structured systems design?

RQ S3-15 What are the structured systems design goals?

RQ S3-16 How might an accountant participate in structured systems design?

RQ S3-17 What are the primary inputs to structured systems design?

RQ S3-18 What does the approved systems design document specify? What is each major component, and what does each component include?

DISCUSSION QUESTIONS

DQ S3-1 "Some organizations contract for 'facilities management' so as not to skew their employee salary structure and elicit the employee dissatisfaction that might result therefrom." Speculate as to the meaning of this statement.

DQ S3-2 "Choosing among renting, leasing, and purchasing computer hardware is strictly a financial decision and should be done by the finance staff." Do you agree? Discuss fully.

DQ S3-3 Apollo Company requests bids from hardware vendors for specific configurations rather than bids for general performance objectives because it knows what it needs. Discuss fully.

DQ S3-4 "An organization puts itself at a disadvantage by asking only one vendor (versus asking several vendors) for a proposal for software or hardware." Do you agree? Discuss fully.

DQ S3-5 "Nobody ever got fired for choosing the market leader for an IT product or service." Comment on this statement in light of the information in this chapter.

DQ S3-6 "Surveys of existing users of software and hardware, such as those published by Dataquest Market Intelligence and Datapro, are biased. Only those users who are very happy or very displeased with their software and/or equipment will respond to such surveys." Discuss fully.

DQ S3-7 Compare and contrast the efficiency and effectiveness of an in-house data center (both centralized and decentralized), an arrangement with an outsourcing vendor to own and operate a data center, a service bureau, and an application service provider (ASP).

DQ S3-8 "As a programmer, I know better than anyone else how to design computer screens and reports, and I am offended when my boss demands that I ask the users what they think should be included in such outputs and how the outputs should be designed." Comment on this statement. Do you agree? Discuss fully.

PROBLEMS

P S3-1 Whippet Insurance Agency is negotiating for the acquisition of computer equipment from JCN Corporation effective January 1, 20XX. Whippet has asked for your assistance in evaluating the available financing alternatives.

One alternative is to purchase the equipment outright for a unit purchase price (UPP) of $120,000 plus 5 percent sales tax, and destination, unpacking, and installation charges estimated at $2,000. The estimated useful life of the equipment is five years, at the end of which the salvage value is estimated at $8,000. If Whippet purchases the equipment it will use straight-line depreciation over a five-year life for tax purposes (instead of the MACRS method). Its marginal income tax rate is 40 percent. For simplicity, assume that the UPP and other out-of-pocket costs will come from existing working capital.

Leasing the equipment through the financing subsidiary of JCN Corporation is another possibility. The key provisions of the lease arrangements include those shown in Exhibit S3.1 (page 97).

Required:

Use spreadsheet software to prepare a comparative analysis of the following financing alternatives, using an approach based on discounted cash flows. Show the *details of each* alternative in two columns: one column for nominal dollars and one for discounted amounts. Use a before-tax discount factor of 12 percent.

a. Outright purchase

b. Lease, with exercise of option to purchase at the end of year 2

c. Lease, with exercise of option to purchase at the end of year 3

d. Lease, with renewal at the end of year 3 and another renewal at the end of year 4

Whenever income tax calculations are required, assume that the cash savings from income taxes occurs at the *end of the year* in which the tax deduction occurs.

Exhibit S3.1 Lease Arrangements for Problem S3-1

Initial lease term:	
Duration[a]	3 years
Monthly lease payment	$4,000
Payable	In arrears at end of each month
Renewal option terms (one-year renewal periods at election of lessee):	
Annual renewal rate as a percent of unit purchase price (UPP):	
Year 4	5 percent
Year 5	3.5 percent
Payable	Annually in advance
Option to purchase—at end of any lease anniversary date, starting with the second anniversary. Purchase option price is a sliding scale, based on UPP, as follows:	
Second lease anniversary	46 percent of UPP
Third anniversary	10 percent of UPP
Fourth and fifth anniversaries	Excluded from consideration[b]
Other charges borne by lessee:	
Destination, unpacking, and installation	$2,000 (estimated)

[a] The lease is written as a "net" lease, wherein the lessee pays for maintenance and casualty insurance. Because these annual expenses would also apply to the purchase alternative, they have been ignored.
[b] Although purchase options beyond the third-year anniversary are available, Whippet has excluded them from consideration.

Personal property taxes are paid at the end of each year by the title holder. The tax rate is $50 per $1,000 of 'value.'" For alternatives b and c, as in the case of the purchase alternative, assume that the option purchase price will come from existing working capital. Also, for cost and personal property tax purposes, consider that the option purchase price is subject to a 5 percent sales tax.

Obtain hard copy printouts of both the results of the calculations and the spreadsheet formulas.

P S3-2 *Note:* In the problem facts, all product and entity names have been disguised. With the exception of these fictitious names, other facts have been modified only slightly from the real-world case from which they were taken.

Facts

Alpha Omega University (AOU) uses a high-end minicomputer, a CHOICE 8950, for its administrative applications and for certain academic applications (teaching and research). Also, faculty and students use between 300 and 350 microcomputers. Three months ago, AOU initiated a search and evaluation process to select microcomputer *communications* software that will serve as a university-wide standard. The next several paragraphs contain *selected* abstracts from the recommendation section of the report by the consultant who evaluated the packages.

Software Selected for Testing

The initial screening of communications packages narrowed the choice to three: REFLECT by Softsell Distributors, Inc., COUPLER by Comsult Company, and COMFOR by Datacom Technologies Corporation. Criteria used in selecting these packages included those in the following table.

Software Comparison Grid

Criteria*	REFLECT	COUPLER	COMFOR
Cost	$69.95	$20.00	$35.00
Ease of use	low	high	high
Vendor support	medium	medium	high
Terminal emulation (SUMS WQ)	yes	no	yes
Modem emulation (Garfield compatible)	yes	yes	yes
Host mode support	yes	no	yes
KERNEL protocol support	yes	no	yes
Line setting flexibility (Luke parity)	no	no	yes
Function key settings	medium	high	low
File transfer performance	excellent	excellent	excellent
Autodial	yes	yes	yes
Transaction/activity log	yes	yes	yes
Shareware	no	yes	yes

*Criteria are not in order of importance.

Final Selection

University Computer User Services (UCUS) supports on-campus communications between microcomputers and the CHOICE 8950. They also support KERNEL v3.3 (a file transfer package), which has been on the CHOICE for approximately one year. Consequently, it was critical that the selected package support the KERNEL protocol. Also, availability of Luke as a parity setting was a highly desirable feature.

The university library has automated its card catalog system with DEWEY. The DEWEY system requires a SUMS WQ terminal emulation. Thus, if users wish to access the DEWEY system from their offices using a microcomputer, the communications package must support this terminal emulation.

By definition, the use of shareware can be risky. Therefore, REFLECT has an advantage in this respect over the other two products. Somewhat offsetting this advantage is the fact that Softsell Distributors is currently involved in a legal suit with RoodTalk Communications (RoodTalk is suing Softsell for copyright infringement).

Required:

a. Using Table S3.2 (page 81) as a guide, prepare a first-level effectiveness analysis of the three competing products. You must decide which software attributes are *mandatory.*

b. For any of the three products that "survive" the first-level effectiveness analysis of part a, construct a *scoring comparison.* Assign weights (totaling 100 points) to each criterion you decide to include in this matrix. Write a brief explanation of why you included each criterion and why you assigned the weight that you did. The following format might be used for your analysis.

Criteria	Weight	REFLECT Value	REFLECT Score	COMFOR Value	COMFOR Score
Criterion 1					
Criterion 2					
Criterion n					
Totals	**100**				

c. Which of the three products do you recommend? Explain your answer. Include a list of other factors, if any, that you might like to investigate *before* making a final recommendation.

P S3-3 Using the Web sites listed in Technology Summary S3.1 (page 78) as a starting point, resolve the following issues:

a. Select sites (or parts of sites) that describe two similar software or hardware products. Write a summary that compares and contrasts the information provided about those products.

b. Select two sites that provide demonstrations of a system. Write a report that compares and contrasts those demos in terms of the functionality and what you are able to learn about the system from the demo.

c. Select two sites that provide tests of a system. Write a report that compares and contrasts those tests in terms of the functionality and what you are able to learn about the system from the test.

P S3-4 Blatcher, Inc., is a manufacturing company that produces mechanical pens. Blatcher purchases raw materials (such as plastic beads that are melted and formed into pen cases, and coiled steel that is twisted and formed into springs) from various vendors. The purchase-pay process works as follows. First, Blatcher has many purchasers who order raw materials from vendors. Each purchase generates a purchase order (PO), on which can be many items. Once the raw materials arrive, a receiver compares the received materials to the PO, checks the quality of the materials, returns defective materials, and places accepted materials in the warehouse. It is possible that the raw materials on a given PO might be received in more than one shipment; meaning, partial shipments are allowed. Meanwhile, the vendor sends an invoice to Blatcher, where one of many accounts payable clerks verifies the PO to the receiving report, time-date stamps the invoice, investigates any discrepancies, and files the documentation in a suspense folder awaiting all receipts and the due date of the invoice. An invoice is not paid until all materials on the original PO have been received. Once the materials have arrived and the due date is near, the accounts payable clerk notifies one of Blatcher's disbursers, who pays for the raw materials on the due date. One check is cut for each PO.

Required:

a. Draw a resources-events-agents (REA) diagram of the purchase-to-pay process at Blatcher, Inc. *Hint:* Refer to Figure S3.3 and the related discussion, and read the following article before attempting to draw the REA diagram—C. L. Dunn and W. E. McCarthy, "The REA Accounting Model: Intellectual Heritage and Prospects for Progress," *Journal of Information Systems* 11 (1) (Spring 1997): 31–51.

b. Referring to Chapter 6 of the textbook, identify the primary keys of each entity in your REA diagram.

c. Referring again to Chapter 6 of the textbook, create any relationship tables that are necessary. *Hint:* Relationship tables are used with many-to-many relationships.

d. From parts a, b, and c, create an entity-relationship diagram and specify all primary and foreign keys. *Hint:* When a primary key from one table (first table) is inserted into a second table (as a way to handle a one-to-many relationship), the primary key of the first table becomes a foreign key in the second table.

KEY TERMS

systems selection

approved configuration
  plan

facilities management

validate

throughput

benchmark

external interviews

software plan

hardware plan

structured systems design

approved systems design
  document

structure chart

module

computer-aided software
  engineering (CASE)

chapter
S4

- To enumerate the goals, plans, tasks, and results of systems implementation.
- To recognize how accountants take part in systems implementation.
- To describe the interdependent tasks that must be accomplished during systems implementation.
- To assess the importance of thoroughly testing the new or revised system prior to putting the system into operation.
- To enumerate the goals, plans, tasks, and results of systems operation.
- To recognize how accountants are involved in systems operation.
- To illustrate the dual functions of post-implementation review, which are to determine the effectiveness and efficiency of the new or revised system and to assess the quality of the development process.
- To analyze the difficulties associated with systems maintenance.

Systems Implementation and Operation

A railroad company called Norfolk Southern Corporation acquired 58 percent of Conrail, and in June 1999 integrated their computer systems.[1] Seven months later they were losing millions of dollars. The IT system generated faulty waybills—instructions on where and when to move individual train cars. As a result, some full trains sat awaiting crews, others were sent back and forth between terminals without being emptied, and empty cars moved along without being filled.

How did this happen? Both Norfolk Southern and Conrail had mainframe software that they had developed in-house. Instead of standardizing on one or the other, or acquiring an *enterprise system* to provide that commonality, they wrote programs to connect the two systems. They spent more than a year coding and testing the interfaces. The CFO at Norfolk Southern admitted that there was insufficient training, erroneous programming, incorrect data conversion, and inadequate system testing—all key components of effective systems implementation. This chapter describes the best practices that lead to successful systems implementation, whether the system is developed in-house (e.g., the systems at Norfolk Southern) or is purchased (e.g., Chapter S1).

---

[1] This story is adapted from Kim S. Nash, "Merged Railroads Still Plagued by IT Snafus," *Computerworld* (January 17, 2000): 20–21.

SYNOPSIS

This chapter concludes the presentation of the systems acquisition and development processes begun in Chapter S1 (AIS acquisition) and continued in Chapters S2 and S3 (internal development and hardware selection). Whether you are dealing with externally acquired or internally developed systems, the concepts and issues in this chapter apply. At this point in the acquisition and development process we may have purchased an AIS (Chapter S1), conducted *systems analysis* to develop the logical specifications and physical requirements for our new or modified information system (Chapter S2), selected hardware for our acquired or developed system (Chapter S3), and completed the systems design and implementation plan (Chapter S3). We are now at the point when it is time to install and begin to use our new or modified system (i.e., *systems implementation*). All the work conducted to date can be for naught if we don't have a successful implementation. For example, prior to using the new system we must carefully test it to make sure that all bugs have been detected.

CONTROLS

ENTERPRISE SYSTEMS

Two important steps in a system's life cycle follow the implementation: post-implementation review and systems maintenance. The former step gives us critical feedback on the quality of the systems acquisition or development process, and of the new system. The latter, systems maintenance, will be necessary no matter how well we conducted systems development. Change happens! We must undertake maintenance in a cost-effective and controlled manner. As we discuss these three systems development steps, we will point out the important controls and the implications of performing these steps to the successful implementation of enterprise systems.

INTRODUCTION

In this chapter, we discuss and illustrate the fifth, sixth, and seventh steps in the systems development life cycle—systems implementation, post-implementation review, and systems maintenance (see bubble numbers 5.0, 6.0, and 7.0 in Figure S4.1).

First, systems implementation includes completing the design[2] of the new or revised system and beginning to use that system. Second, post-implementation review assesses the adequacy of the new system vis-à-vis the user's requirements and the quality of the acquisition/development process. Third, systems maintenance involves making repairs and modifications to the system. While we briefly mentioned some screen and report formatting issues in Chapter S3, we further examine these important issues in Appendix S4, which describes detailed guidelines for the design of effective reports, documents, and screens.

Recall from Chapters S2 and S3 that certain systems development tasks are comparable to those undertaken in the planning and construction of an industrial park. *Systems implementation* (in which the computer programs are written, the design of the database and documents is finalized, and the system is put into operation) is analogous to the process of actually constructing the industrial park. *Post-implementation review*, in which the organization checks to see that the system does what it was supposed to do,

[2] In this chapter, we include some "design" activities that other people would argue belong in earlier steps of the SDLC. We do not want to debate where design ends and execution of the design begins. You should recognize that design is a continuum as opposed to a discrete function. We *complete* our design work in this chapter.

Figure S4.1 Systems Development Life Cycle

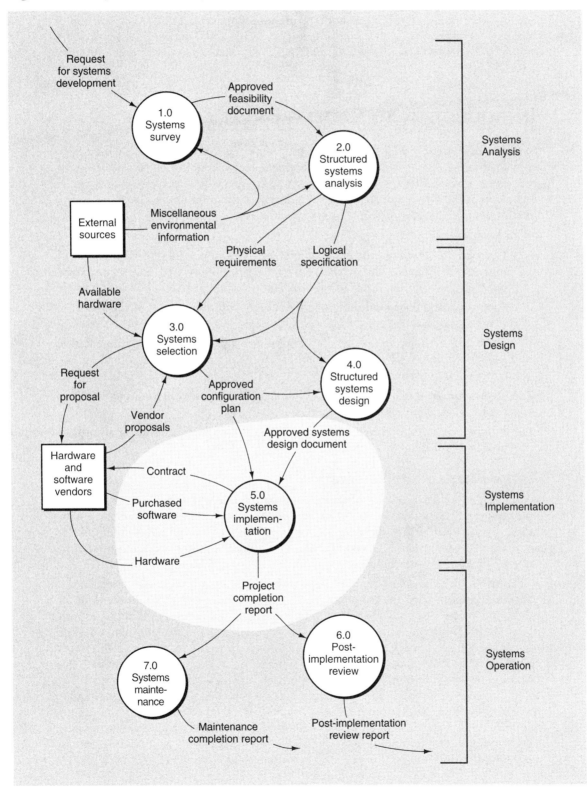

is similar to the building inspection that occurs soon after the industrial park is completed. *Systems maintenance*, in which system errors are corrected and enhancements are added to the system, is similar to undertaking plumbing or electrical repairs or minor building modifications, such as moving interior walls and relocating doors. Systems maintenance, like building repairs and modifications, usually takes place on an ongoing basis.

INTRODUCTION TO SYSTEMS IMPLEMENTATION

Systems implementation reflects a set of procedures performed to *complete* the design contained in the *approved systems design document* and to test, install, and begin to use the new or revised information system. Figure S4.1 (page 103) depicts systems implementation as the fifth major step in the development of an information system. Examine this figure to see the position that systems implementation holds in the SDLC.

The *systems implementation goals* are as follows:

- Complete, as necessary, the design contained in the approved systems design document. For example, the detailed contents of new or revised documents, computer screens, and the database must be laid out and created.

- Write, test, and document the programs and procedures required by the approved systems design document.

- Ensure, by completing the preparation of user manuals and other documentation and by educating and training personnel, that the organization's personnel can operate the new system.

- Determine, by thoroughly testing the system with users, that the system satisfies the users' requirements.

- Ensure a correct conversion by planning, controlling, and conducting an orderly installation of the new system.

Approaches to Implementation

In this section we describe implementation approaches that can be taken to install whatever portion of the system that has been developed. Selecting an appropriate implementation approach can greatly facilitate conversion to the new system. Depending on the approach and circumstances, greater control and user satisfaction can be ensured. Figure S4.2 depicts the three most common implementation approaches.

CONTROLS   Figure S4.2(a), the *parallel approach*, provides the most control of the three. In the **parallel approach**, both the old and new systems operate together for a time. During this period—time *x* to time *y* (which is usually one operating cycle, such as one month or one quarter)—the outputs of the two systems are compared to determine whether the new system is operating comparably to the old. At time *y*, management makes a decision, based on the comparison of the two systems' outputs, whether to terminate the operation of the old system. The parallel approach provides a high level of control because the old system is not abandoned until users are satisfied that the new system adequately replaces the old. However, greater control comes at a cost; meaning, it is expensive to keep two systems running simultaneously. For instance, running two systems side-by-side can require duplicate or excess computer processing capacity, data storage space, and human labor.

Figure S4.2 **Implementation Approaches**

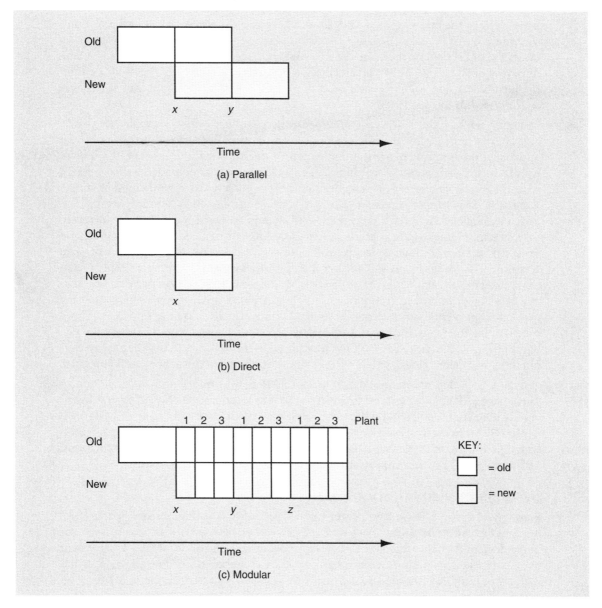

Figure S4.2(b), the **direct approach**, is the riskiest of the three approaches because at time *x* the old system is stopped and the new system is begun. This implementation method is also referred to as the *big bang* or *cold turkey approach*. There can be no validation that the new system operates comparably to the old because the lights are turned off with the old system and simultaneously turned on with the new system. *Enterprise systems* are often implemented using this approach. Direct implementations can lead to disaster if not carefully planned and executed. So, why take this approach? Certainly, some level of comfort or control is lost with the direct approach. But, this implementation method can be less costly than the parallel approach—if all goes well. With very

ENTERPRISE SYSTEMS

CONTROLS

large implementations, such as enterprise systems, it is often capacity and/or cost prohibitive to take the parallel approach. On the bright side, the direct approach forces users to learn the new system, as they do not have the old system to fall back on. While this might have immediate negative effects on satisfaction, since users do not want to let go of the old system or they fear the new system, the new system can get up and running very quickly. And, if the implementation is properly planned and the users are thoroughly trained, direct implementations can ultimately lead to increased user satisfaction as compared to the old system.

CONTROLS   Figure S4.2(c), the *modular approach*, can be combined with the parallel or the direct approaches to tailor the implementation to the circumstances. With the **modular approach**, the new system is either implemented one subsystem or module at a time or is introduced one organizational unit at a time. The modular approach is also referred to as the *phased approach*. For example, a new order entry/sales system could be implemented by first changing the sales order preparation and customer inquiry portions, followed by implementing the link to the billing system, followed by the link to the inventory system. Figure S4.2(c) depicts the gradual implementation of a new system into three organizational units. A new payroll system is installed for the employees of plant 1 at time *x*, followed by plant 2 at time *y*, and finally by plant 3 at time *z*. Implementation at any plant could be direct or parallel. Modular implementation permits *pilot testing* of a system or system component and elimination of any problems discovered before full implementation. If properly planned and executed, modular implementations can combine the safety and control of a parallel implementation with the cost/time savings of a direct approach. Technology Application S4.1 overviews how Walt Disney Corporation managed a global SAP implementation using the modular or phased approach.

ENTERPRISE SYSTEMS   Figure S4.3 depicts the modular schedule used at Boston Scientific Corporation to implement SAP at all of its worldwide divisions and locations. As shown, several installations have been completed while two more are scheduled for the end of March. At Boston Scientific, several members of the project team were on location for each worldwide "go live" date to provide assistance, to ensure consistency of all implementations, and to learn and provide improvements for subsequent implementations.

Systems Implementation Plans

Figure S4.4 (page 108), a lower-level view of process 5.0 in Figure S4.1 (page 103), outlines the *systems implementation tasks and documents* necessary to achieve the systems implementation goals presented earlier. After we discuss the accountant's involvement in systems implementation, we will describe each component in Figure S4.4, starting with the output, then the inputs, and finally the intermediate steps (bubbles 5.1 through 5.8).

THE ACCOUNTANT'S INVOLVEMENT IN SYSTEMS IMPLEMENTATION

We find that the accountant could play one of several roles (first introduced in Table S1.2 on page 9) in the systems implementation step. As an analyst, the accountant could be the development team member who completes the systems design, or the programmer who codes the computer programs. As a consultant, the accountant could be called in to complete the design; help prepare the contracts; or help plan, conduct, and evaluate the

Technology Application S4.1

Walt Disney Corporation's Global SAP Implementation

Walt Disney Corporation (Disney) embarked on a major SAP implementation in 2001, code named Project Tomorrowland. The scale of the project was enormous, as Disney planned to integrate 400 back-end office systems into a single SAP platform. While the total cost of the project was expected to be around $390 million, ongoing annual cost savings were anticipated to be in the vicinity of $125 million. A simple payback calculation of slightly over three years revealed the significant potential value of this project. However, because the implementation involved many locations, people, and processes, Disney had to very carefully plan and execute the global roll-out. Phase one of the implementation, involving U.S. corporate offices, was finished on time and within budget. The second phase, which was to implement SAP at the Disneyland theme park, also ran relatively flawlessly. The third and most aggressive phase was to implement SAP at Disney UK, Disney's European headquarters, and Walt Disney World. Just before the third phase began, major problems emerged from the first two phases. Most significantly, a major programming error surfaced in Disney's internally developed accounting system, poor quality control over data conversion resulted in an error-prone payroll system, and key reports were not being provided to managers. The implementation team deduced that the primary cause of these problems could be traced to a lack of executive and user involvement at local levels. Once the noted problems were fixed, the implementation team changed policies so that, most notably, local executives and key users became much more involved in the implementation process. As a result, Disney averted potential disaster and phase three of the implementation was successful. This example illustrates how the modular or phased implementation approach detected major problems early enough in the implementation to allow for corrective procedural changes before continuing with the project.

Source: Mike Simons, "Disney Keeps Global SAP Roll-out on Track by Making Local Executives Responsible," *Computerweekly.com* (July 1, 2003).

Figure S4.3 Boston Scientific Global Roll-Out Schedule

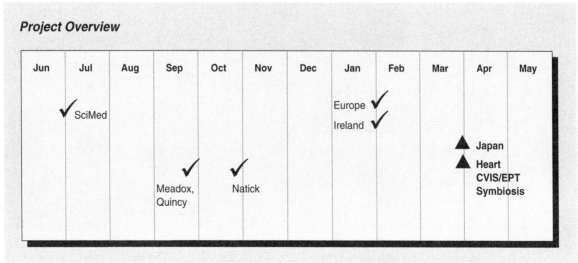

Source: Reprinted with permission from Dave Ellard, Vice President, Global Systems, Boston Scientific Corporation.

Figure S4.4 Systems Implementation Tasks and Documents

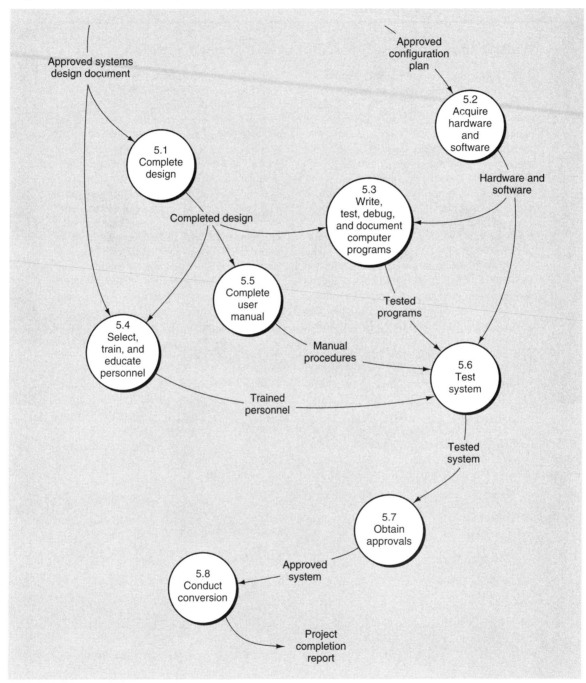

system tests. As a user (e.g., staff accountant or business process owner), he can become deeply involved in systems implementation, especially when an accounting system is being implemented. A staff accountant could be the project leader and have control over the final design, testing, and acceptance of the new system. As a member of the implementation team, the staff accountant could help design system inputs and outputs or specify testing criteria. Whether or not a team member, the staff accountant might be a system user, and thus would be trained in the use of the new system. Finally, the internal auditor/IT auditor would evaluate conversion plans and conversion test results and would review systems development documentation for completeness and conformity to organization standards.

THE SYSTEMS IMPLEMENTATION DELIVERABLE: THE PROJECT COMPLETION REPORT

Systems implementation ends with the operation of the newly acquired or revised system and with the submission of the project completion report. The **project completion report** summarizes the implementation activities and provides documentation for operating the new system and for conducting the post-implementation review and systems maintenance. The project completion report usually includes the following items:

- Summary of requirements satisfied by the new system.
- Estimated and actual duration of each development stage.
- Estimated and actual systems performance (e.g., response time, costs, benefits).
- *System documentation*, which provides an overview of the new system.
- *Program documentation*, which includes source code and other related items.
- *User manual*, which describes operating procedures for both manual and automated procedures.
- *Operations run manual*, which contains operating instructions for computer operations.
- System test report.
- User training programs and manuals.
- Operator training programs and manuals.

TRIGGERING SYSTEMS IMPLEMENTATION

In Figure S4.1 (page 103), you can see that systems implementation follows *structured systems design* and has as its two major inputs the *approved configuration plan*, developed during the *systems selection* step, and the *approved systems design document*, produced in the *structured systems design* step of systems development. Recall from Chapter S3 that the approved configuration plan specifies the software and hardware to be used with the new or revised system. During systems implementation, the organization acquires the specified computer resources, prepares the site to receive them, and installs the new software and hardware. Also recall from Chapter S3 that the approved systems design document contains the design specifications, the implementation plan, the implementation test plan, the initial elements of the user manual, and the training plan. During systems implementation, the approved systems design document is used to complete the design, write the computer programs, conduct the training, test the system, and install the new or revised system.

THE INTERMEDIATE STEPS IN SYSTEMS IMPLEMENTATION

Complete the Design

During systems implementation, we need to complete the design of input and output reports, documents, computer screens, the database, manual processes, and certain computer processes (Figure S4.4, bubble 5.1, page 108). System outputs, usually the objective of the development project, are designed first, and followed by inputs, then the database, and finally processes. These specifications are required whether we purchase or develop a new system. Acquired systems must be configured to provide the tailored functionality required by the users. We now proceed with a brief description of how the input, output, database, and report designs are completed.

Data required for output must be entered or generated by the application's process steps (e.g., a calculated amount) or retrieved from other previously stored data. In designing the system, the analyst/designer must decide the best method for providing the elements included in the application's outputs. Appendix S4 provides guidelines for the design of effective system components, including reports, documents, and computer screens.

In addition to designing the application's outputs and inputs, the development team must lay out its database. This layout depicts a *logical* view of each database record and indicates the field (i.e., attribute) names and lengths. The *database administrator (DBA)* uses this layout to map the logical record into storage. The DBA must decide where and how to store each data element.

Finally, the specifications for the manual and automated processes must be completed at this time. The specifications for each computer program module must be adequate for the writing of the computer program code. The manual procedures must contain sufficient detail to allow for the writing of the procedures manuals.

Acquire Hardware and Software

At any time after the computer resources are chosen and indicated in the *approved configuration plan*, the software and hardware may be acquired (Figure S4.4, bubble 5.2, page 108), the site prepared, and the computer system installed.

Contract negotiation and preparation is an important part of the computer acquisition process. Computer, legal, and financial expertise must be combined to negotiate and execute the contracts. Contracts are necessary for computer hardware lease, rental, or purchase; for software lease, rental, or purchase; and for hardware and software service, such as a *systems integrator*, a *service bureau*, or an *application service provider*. The important point to remember when contracts are negotiated is that nothing should be left out of the contract; nothing should be assumed. Detailed specifications protect the buyer and the seller and keep them both out of court, unless one fails to perform contract provisions. Technology Excerpt S4.1 provides some contract preparation guidelines.

The site to receive the computer equipment must be prepared carefully. Sufficient electrical power and power protection, air conditioning, and security, as well as the computer room's physical structure and access to that room, must be planned for and provided. If the contracts are well written and the site well prepared, installation of the computer hardware, software, and related equipment should be relatively straightforward.

Technology Excerpt S4.1

Guidelines for Preparing Contracts for Computing Resources

The following guidelines regarding contracts for computer hardware, software, and computing services come from experienced users of IT.

- Be cautious of a vendor contract that goes to great lengths to tell you what the vendor *won't* do.
- Be clear on what *is* being provided by the vendor, including measurable service levels and availability.
- Obtain vendor warranties for intellectual property infringements, third-party indemnification, and nonconforming services. Determine the remedies for failure to meet contracted obligations.
- For a consulting engagement, include the names of the people who will work on the project and set a maximum turnover rate.
- Include a detailed project plan that lists what will be delivered, when it will be delivered, and how it will perform.
- Tie payments to completion of project phases and acceptance of deliverables, such as software, hardware, documentation, and training.
- Obtain the services of a procurement professional to ensure consistency across contracts and to provide an independent viewpoint in contract negotiations.
- If you want to make changes to source code or have a third-party make changes, include this right in the contract.

Sources: Joe Auer, "Who Gets the Risk? And Who Ducks It?" *Computerworld* (June 26, 2000): 78; Kim S. Nash, "Users Say Consultants Play Role in IT Disasters," *Computerworld* (November 6, 2000): 20; Joe Auer, "Work Out Details Later? No! Now!" *Computerworld* (November 13, 2000): 90; Jaikumar Vijayan, "Court OKs Third-Party Software Maintenance," *Computerworld* (June 26, 2000): 4.

Contingency plans to allow for delays in site preparation or equipment delivery should be considered.

Write, Test, Debug, and Document Computer Programs

The next task in systems implementation is to write the computer programs, test and debug the programs, and complete the program documentation (Figure S4.4, bubble 5.3, page 108). The programming process is important because the programming task in systems development consumes more resources and time than any other development task. Although many of you are familiar with the programming process, let us review a few of its important elements.[3]

The programmer must develop the test plan, which outlines how each program module will be tested. The test plan includes the test data that the program unit is expected to handle. The user, the programmer, and another member of the programming team do a "walkthrough" of the module specifications and the test plan to determine that the latter is adequate; then the programmer codes the program. Or the code might be created by computer software (a code generator) that "writes" program code. At least two programmers then do a walkthrough of the code to see that the code faithfully and without

---

[3] We will only review these elements because a detailed coverage of programming, program testing, and debugging is beyond the scope of this text. However, do not be deceived by the brevity of this section. In addition to consuming more time and resources than any other development task, programming can be fraught with problems. However, the use of *structured* design techniques can alleviate many of the problems of translating a program's specifications into a production version of the program.

error implements the module specifications. The programmer tests the individual module and removes any errors found during testing. Because these errors are called *bugs*, the removal of program errors is called *debugging*. Finally, the programmer must complete the program documentation. *Maintenance* programmers will use this documentation to make program changes, correct errors in the programs, and add enhancements to the programs.

ENTERPRISE SYSTEMS

If a software package has been purchased, much of the programming step is replaced with procedures to configure the system for this application. During the implementation of an *enterprise system*, this process can be quite extensive as we configure the system to select, for example, the steps to be completed for each business process; the design of the screens to be displayed at each step of the process; and the data to be captured, stored, and output during the processes. Much programming may remain, however. To tie the new ERP modules to the legacy systems, program code must be written—in ABAP for SAP and C++ for J.D. Edwards, for example. While not ERP systems, programs were written to link the legacy systems at Norfolk Southern and Conrail.

Select, Train, and Educate Personnel

The organization must choose the personnel who will operate the new system and must train them to perform their system-related duties (Figure S4.4, bubble 5.4, page 108). As noted at the beginning of the chapter, the insufficient training of the system users at Norfolk Southern was one of the factors leading to the failure to successfully implement the merged Norfolk Southern/Conrail systems. The system's users must be educated about the new system's purpose, function, and capabilities. In determining who to train and how much training to deliver, the organization might conduct a cost/benefit analysis to determine the cost associated with *not* training. Training may be given through a combination of schools run by software vendors, hardware vendors, vendors specializing in training, and programs conducted by the organization itself. Computer-assisted learning, such as interactive tutorials, might also be used.

An organization must choose the training delivery system that matches its training needs. The two variables to be considered in choosing a delivery method are the person being trained and the training objective. For example, formal classroom presentations, delivered to any audience, are appropriate for general overviews of a computer system. On-the-job training can be an effective *component* of a plan that includes instruction, follow-up, and ongoing assistance. Videotapes convey, in a consistent manner, information to a geographically dispersed audience and can be another effective element of a training program. Tutorials introduce relatively computer-literate users to software and hardware utilization. Without assistance, tutorials can be difficult for novices to use.

E-BUSINESS

ENTERPRISE SYSTEMS

Computer-based training (CBT) provides learning via computer directly to the trainee's computer screen. Training may be delivered over the Internet by vendors whose business it is to design, produce, and deliver such training. ERP vendors, such as SAP and J.D. Edwards, have created extensive CBT programs to help users learn the extensive features of their systems. CBT can be 20 to 25 percent less expensive than lectures, and it also permits individualized instruction, which can take place when and where needed. The interactive nature of CBT can get and keep a trainee's attention. However, some employees, particularly middle and senior management, prefer more personal, traditional delivery methods.

Resident experts may be a cost-effective way to deliver knowledge of a system to a large audience. In such situations, the experts are trained first and then they instruct the other users. Peer teaching may also be more effective than using professional instructors, particularly when *cyberphobia*—the fear of computers—is strong. Online HELP and EX-PLANATION facilities, along with well-designed screens and reports, can reduce the amount of up-front training necessary and provide ongoing guidance to system users.

Complete User Manual

A *user manual* should describe operating procedures for both manual and automated systems functions (Figure S4.4, bubble 5.5, page 108). The manual should cover user responsibilities, system inputs, computer system interfaces, manual files and databases, controls (including error detection and correction), distribution and use of system outputs, and manual and automated processing instructions. Good user manuals can improve system efficiency and effectiveness. If users know how to utilize a system properly and they employ it willingly, the system will be used correctly, more frequently, more productively, and will better meet users' needs.

The systems designer, the user, and possibly the organization's technical writing and training staff should cooperate in preparing the user manual. Because the systems designer knows intimately what the system will do, she is well qualified to describe how to use the system. The systems designer should begin preparing the user manual as the detailed system specifications are developed.

The user, who must study the manual to learn the system and then keep the manual as a reference for continued operation of the system, must make sure that the manual is relevant for the tasks to be performed and that it is complete, accurate, and clear.

The organization's training staff should be involved in preparing the manual because they must train users to operate the new system. The staff must learn the system themselves and develop separate training materials and/or utilize the user manual as the training vehicle. Therefore, they are very interested in, and should have input to, developing the user manual. Exhibit S4.1 (page 114) is an excerpt from a typical user manual.

Test System

Beyond testing program modules, the entire system is tested to determine that it meets the requirements established by the business process owners and users and that it can be used and operated to the satisfaction of both users and system operators (Figure S4.4, bubble 5.6, page 108). Testing is carried out by the systems developers, by the developers and the users together, and finally by the users. The more closely the test can simulate a production environment (e.g., people, machines, data, inputs), the more representative the test will be and the more conclusive the results will be. At Norfolk Southern the system tests were conducted using pristine data and could not, therefore, determine how the systems would react to erroneous data. Each test consists of the following steps:

CONTROLS

- Specify test conditions.
- Review test conditions (i.e., walkthrough).
- Create test data.
- Execute tests.
- Evaluate results.

Several types or levels of tests are usually completed before a system can be implemented. From the users' point of view, three of these tests are the most important. The **system test** verifies the new system against the original specifications. This test is conducted first by the development team and then by the users with the assistance of the

Exhibit S4.1 Sample User Manual Instructions for Sales Order Input

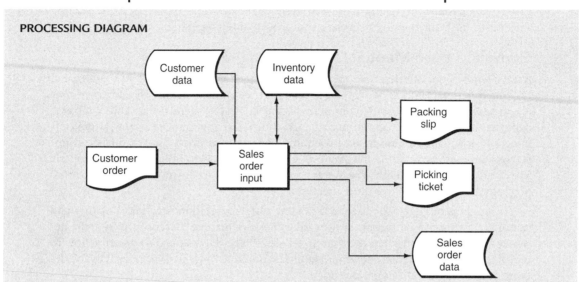

PROCESSING OVERVIEW

The sales order input program receives online input of customer orders, creates a sales order record, allocates inventory in the inventory data, prints a packing slip on the shipping office printer, and prints a picking ticket on the warehouse printer.

PROCESSING OBJECTIVES

The input is edited. It is compared to the inventory data and the customer data to ensure accuracy and to ensure that the customer and inventory items exist. It is compared to the customer's credit record (in the customer data) to ensure the customer's creditworthiness. Totals are calculated to ensure accurate and complete input. All this is done quickly, ensuring timely processing of the customer order.

PROCESSING TASKS

1. Receive batches of customer orders from a sales order supervisor.
2. Log on to the system using your password.
3. Select sales order system.
4. Select sales order input.

5. Key batch totals (number of customer orders, hash total of customer order numbers, arithmetic total of items ordered).
6. Key each order as follows:

   (Specific input instructions with sample screens would be included.)
7. After each batch is completed:

   (A description of how to "agree" the batch totals and release the batch for processing would be included.)

ERROR-CORRECTING PROCEDURES

1. If customer record is not found: Remove customer order from the batch, recalculate the batch total, and return the customer order to the supervisor.

   (A description of how to handle each error would be included.)

HELP PROCEDURES

If you cannot determine what the problem is, seek help from your supervisor, or call user support at ext. 2207.

team. The **acceptance test** is a *user*-directed test of the complete system in a test environment. The purpose is to determine, from the user's perspective, whether all components of the new system are satisfactory. The user tests the adequacy of the system (both manual and automated components), of the manuals and other documentation, and of the training the users received. Finally, the **operations test** or **environmental test** runs a subset of the system in the actual production environment. This final test determines whether new equipment and other factors in the environment—such as data entry areas, document and report deliveries, telephones, and electricity—are satisfactory.

As noted earlier, *enterprise systems* are often implemented using a *direct* or "big bang" approach. Successful implementations often involve extensive testing. For example, before implementing SAP at Lucent Technologies, Inc., more than 70 business users tested the system for six months. At the Gillette Company 150 workers ran test transactions for four months.[4]

ENTERPRISE SYSTEMS

Obtain Approvals

The *project completion report* is approved as follows (Figure S4.4, bubble 5.7, page 108):

- Users verify that the system, including the user manual, meets their requirements. Users also approve conversion and training plans to confirm that these plans are adequate.

- IT confirms that the system has been completed and that it works. IT also approves the training and conversion plans. Finally, IT performs a technical review of the system to determine that acceptable design and programming standards have been applied.

- Management reviews the systems performance objectives, cost, and projected benefits to ensure that implementation is consistent with the best interests of the organization.

- IT auditors compare test results with the original system requirements and specifications to determine that the system has been tested and will operate satisfactorily. IT auditors are also interested in the adequacy of controls within the system and the controls identified for the conversion process. Finally, IT auditors confirm that the development team followed the organization's systems development standards.

CONTROLS

Conduct Conversion

After all the previous design steps have been completed and signed off, the organization must carefully convert to the new system (Figure S4.4, bubble 5.8, page 108). Conversion includes converting the data, converting the processes (i.e., the programs), and completing the documentation. Controls must be in place to ensure the accurate, complete, and authorized conversion of the data and programs.

CONTROLS

As the existing data are mapped into the new system, exception-reporting situations must be devised to ensure that the data are converted accurately. At Norfolk Southern the data used on the go-live date was old data that had been used for testing. The user must suggest control totals that can be used to test the completeness and accuracy of the data conversion. For example, the total number of inventory items, the total on-hand quantity for all inventory items, or a *hash total* of inventory item numbers might be used as totals.

Boston Scientific (see Figure S4.3, page 107) implemented SAP over the course of two years at each of its worldwide divisions and locations (i.e., a *modular approach*). But since SAP was implemented using the *direct approach* at each of those locations, the data conversion was tested at least *seven* times, until there were no errors! They believe that this testing was the key to the successful implementations.[5]

ENTERPRISE SYSTEMS

---

[4] Craig Stedman, "ERP Requires Exhaustive Full-System Tests," *Computerworld* (November 8, 1999): 38.
[5] Dave Ellard, Vice President, Global Systems, Boston Scientific, "Global Systems in 18 Months," presentation, Bentley College, Waltham, MA, March 20, 2000.

Both manual and computer-based processes must be converted. Conversion to new computer programs must be undertaken using *program change controls* to ensure that only authorized, tested, and approved versions of the programs are promoted to production status.

The systems development project team now writes the *project completion report*, the final step in the implementation process. As discussed earlier, this report includes a summary of conversion activities and information with which to operate and maintain the new system.

SYSTEMS OPERATION

An organization should periodically examine the system in its production environment to determine whether the system is continuing to satisfy the user's needs. If the system possibly can be made to work better, its value to the user will increase. There are three different types of periodic examination:

1. The *post-implementation review* is conducted to follow up a system's recent implementation. This review is analogous to a follow-up examination that a doctor might perform after a recent operation.

2. *Systems maintenance*, performed in response to a specific request, is conducted if the system has a relatively minor deficiency. This examination is similar to one a doctor performs on sick people.

3. The periodic *systems survey* is undertaken whenever it is likely that the costs of the review will be less than the value of the improvements that the review will suggest. This reevaluation is like a periodic physical examination that we might ask our doctor to perform.

Figure S4.5 shows that the post-implementation review is the sixth major step of the SDLC, systems maintenance is the seventh step, and the systems survey is the first step. The post-implementation review and systems maintenance are discussed in the next two sections.

The Post-Implementation Review

The **post-implementation review** involves an examination of a working information system, conducted soon after that system's implementation. The post-implementation review determines whether the user's requirements have been satisfied and whether the development effort was efficient and conducted in accordance with the organization's systems development standards. The post-implementation review should be brief and inexpensive. Examinations conducted in response to a specific deficiency, systems maintenance, are discussed in the next section.

The *post-implementation review goals* are as follows:

- Determine whether the user is satisfied with the new system.
- Identify the degree of correspondence between system performance requirements and the system's achieved performance.
- Evaluate the quality of the new system's documentation, training programs, and data conversions.
- Review the performance of the new system and, if necessary, recommend improvements.

Figure S4.5 Systems Development Life Cycle

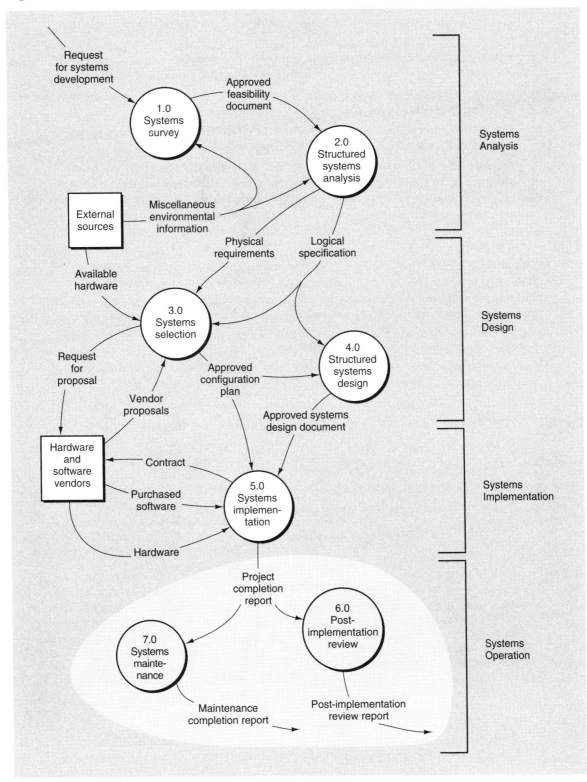

- Ascertain that the organization's project management framework and SDLC were followed during development.
- Recommend improvements to the systems development standards manual if necessary.
- Perfect the cost/effectiveness analysis process by reviewing cost projections and benefit estimations and determining the degree to which these were achieved.
- Perfect project-planning procedures by examining total project costs and the project team's ability to adhere to project cost estimates and schedules.
- Make any other recommendations that might improve the operation of the system or the development of other information systems.

CONTROLS   Internal auditors, IT auditors, or systems analysts (other than those who developed the system) may conduct the post-implementation review. If the organization has insufficient personnel with the required expertise who are independent of the system's development, consultants may be hired to conduct the review. The independence of the review is important because the review provides feedback (i.e., a control) on the development process.

The post-implementation review is performed as soon as the system is operating at full capacity, which could be one month or one year after implementation. The review should examine a fully functioning system so as not to draw erroneous conclusions about system performance. The review should be conducted soon enough after implementation to be able to take advantage of any improvements that can be made to the system or to the systems development methods used.

The **post-implementation review report** contains the review team's conclusions and recommendations. The report usually includes the items described in Exhibit S4.2.

Exhibit S4.2 Typical Contents of the Post-Implementation Review Report

1. The system goals and an indication of how well the system meets those goals.
2. An assessment of the system's overall quality.
3. An assessment of the quality of the development process.
4. Conclusions and recommendations, including the following:
   a. Recommendations for improving the performance of the new system. If the system does not meet user needs or is for some other reason found deficient, systems maintenance may be recommended to repair the deficiencies, or additional training may be suggested to improve the level of user knowledge regarding the system's operation. If there are dramatic problems, the review team could advise that a systems survey be conducted to evaluate the need for a more radical system repair.
   b. Recommendations for improving the project management and systems development processes. If the systems development effort is found to be deficient, the systems development team may be disciplined or may receive additional training. If the project management framework or systems development methodology (i.e., the systems development standards manual) is found to be deficient, the methodology should be corrected.

CONTROLS   The following parties *sign off* on the post-implementation review report:

- Business process owners/users sign off to indicate that the system was performing as depicted in the report and to indicate concurrence with the report's conclusions and recommendations.

- Auditors participating in the review sign off to indicate that appropriate procedures were followed in performing the review and to concur with the report's conclusions and recommendations.

Systems Maintenance

Systems maintenance is the modification (e.g., repair, correction, or enhancement) of existing applications. Systems maintenance expenditures can account for 50 to 70 percent of the total cost of a system over its total life cycle. For example, 80 percent of the total cost of software is in maintenance.[6] These costs should be reason enough to reduce the need for maintenance and to carefully monitor maintenance that cannot be avoided.

You should realize that not all maintenance expense is necessarily bad; rather, the issue is the *relative* amount spent on systems maintenance. After all, applications must be adapted to a changing environment and improved over time. There are three types of maintenance activities:

1. *Corrective* maintenance must be performed to fix errors.

2. *Perfective* maintenance is conducted to improve the performance of an application.

3. *Adaptive* maintenance adjusts applications to reflect changing business needs and environmental challenges.

The competitiveness of many industries and the need for organizations to remain flexible in such environments increase the importance of adaptive maintenance.

The following *systems maintenance goals* are established in light of the systems maintenance costs and concerns cited, as well as other issues to be discussed in this section:

- Accomplish system changes quickly and efficiently.
- Prevent system changes from causing other system problems.
- Make system changes that are in the organization's overall best interest.
- Perfect systems development and systems maintenance procedures by collecting and using information about system changes.
- Supplant systems maintenance with the systems survey if requested changes are significant or if they would destroy the system (i.e., would be the straw that broke the camel's back).
- Minimize control exposure and organizational disruption that can be caused by systems maintenance.

To accomplish the systems maintenance goals, organizations often adopt the following procedures and controls for their systems maintenance process:

CONTROLS

- Because systems maintenance is like a miniature systems development, it should include analysis, cost/benefit study, design, implementation, and approvals for each development step. In systems maintenance, certain SDLC procedures deserve more attention than others. For example, changes must be tested prior to implementation to determine that a change corrects the problem and does not cause other problems. Participants and signoffs should be the same as those required for systems development. For example, the user should review system changes.

- By charging users for maintenance costs, an organization can reduce the submission of frivolous maintenance requests.

---

[6] Carol Sliwa, "Web Site Upgrades: Build or Buy?" *Computerworld* (January 17, 2000): 16; "Sizing Up the SDLC," Gartner Group Research Note QA-05-9636, October 29, 1998.

- By adopting a formal procedure for submitting change requests, batching these requests together for each application, and then prioritizing the batches, management can gain control of systems maintenance and reduce the expense and disruptions caused by the maintenance process.

- During systems maintenance, information should be gathered that provides feedback to improve the operation of the system and to improve the systems development process. For instance, poor-quality application documentation and inadequate user training can cause numerous systems maintenance requests. Correcting these deficiencies can preclude the need for similar maintenance requests in the future. Likewise, improvements in the systems development process can prevent deficiencies from occurring in other systems when they are being developed.

- Management should see that *program change controls* (see Chapter 8, especially Figure 8.6, in the accompanying textbook) are used to ensure that all modifications to computer programs are authorized, tested, and properly implemented.

- High-quality documentation must be created and maintained. Without current, accurate documentation, maintenance programmers cannot understand, and therefore cannot effectively or efficiently modify, existing programs.

CONTROLS   In addition to these systems maintenance procedures and controls, management should consider adoption of the following policies and procedures, which might relieve the systems maintenance problem:

- Require that auditors conduct audits of the SDLC and of the operation of application systems to reduce development problems and to assess *operations system* effectiveness and efficiency.

- Reduce user-requested system modifications by increasing user familiarity with, knowledge of, and sophistication in the use of application systems.

- Convert programs that are difficult to maintain from conventional languages to those that are easier to maintain.

The **maintenance completion report** documents the systems maintenance process. It usually contains the items described in Exhibit S4.3.

Exhibit S4.3 Typical Contents of the Maintenance Completion Report

1. The completed systems change request form, including an explanation of the requested change, a justification for the change, and user and management approvals.

2. An explanation of action taken on the request.

3. Documentation of changes made, including, as required, new flowcharts, DFDs, E-R diagrams, logic specifications, user and operator manuals, and so on.

4. Test procedures and results.

5. Recommendations for other changes that the system may require, recommendations for improvements to the systems development process that might preclude subsequent systems development shortcomings, and suggestions for user training that might improve user participation in systems development projects and reduce the users' need to modify existing systems.

6. Final systems maintenance approvals, including those of the users, the systems analysts, the designers who conducted the maintenance, management, IT management, and auditors.

Summary

In this chapter we have discussed the final three steps in the *systems development life cycle*: systems implementation, post-implementation review, and systems maintenance. As we have discussed these steps, we have emphasized the impact that the successful completion of these steps has on the achievement of the systems development objectives (i.e., system meets user needs, efficient and effective systems development process).

There may be, however, another twist on this cause and effect relationship.[7] At the time we have implemented a system and conducted the post-implementation review, we might measure the development process as successful. That is, we have delivered a system that meets most of the user requirements, we have implemented the system on time and within budget, and there does not seem to be any bugs. These are all short-term measures.

It is not until we conduct systems maintenance that we discover that the system has some long-term faults. It may not be, for example, flexible, scalable, reliable, or maintainable. These faults drive up the life cycle cost of the system and cause maintenance costs to be 50 to 70 percent of the long-term costs. The solution is to incorporate the long-term requirements (e.g., flexibility, maintainability) into the initial user requirements and to measure the success of the implementation over the long run, rather than at the time of the implementation.

APPENDIX S4

Report, Document, and Screen Layout

In this appendix, we discuss the general considerations for input and output design and the specific design considerations for three media used for input and output: reports, display screens, and business forms. Inputs should be designed so as to facilitate accurate capture of input data and conversion of those data to machine-readable form. Exhibit S4.4 enumerates some general considerations for input design. Exhibit S4.5 enumerates some general considerations for output design.

Documents, often called **forms**, are used internally or externally to capture data that may then be input to a computer. An example is a form used by employees to request reimbursement for items such as travel. Forms also may be used to record systems output. We distinguish output *documents* from output *reports* by the preprinted information contained on output documents (e.g., a company's name, address, etc., would normally be preprinted on a sales invoice by the forms supply company). Forms—documents used to capture data—should meet the following criteria:

- Be easy to complete and use.
- Minimize the errors that can be made in completing a form and keying from a completed form.
- Minimize cost.
- Not contain too much data or be too sparse or too busy.

---

[7] The ideas presented here are derived from Ed Yourdon, "Long-Term Thinking," *Computerworld* (October 16, 2000): 50.

Exhibit S4.4 Input Design Considerations and Guidelines

DECISIONS

- Input format (e.g., free-form, formatted specifically for input)
- Input source (e.g., clerical offices, warehouse/factory, outside organization)
- Source document (e.g., document, report, paper spreadsheet)
- Source document preparer (e.g., customer, sales personnel, clerical staff, management)
- Input operator (e.g., data entry operator, sales personnel, management, customer)
- Input method (e.g., direct keying, OCR, OMR, voice, scanning, bar codes, RFID)
- Timeliness (e.g., input on demand, input daily, input when batch accumulated)

CONTROLS

- Validity (How do we know this is a valid input?)
- Verification (Will the input be verified—e.g., key verified?)
- Audit trail (e.g., customer number input for sales order)
- Batch totals (Will they be calculated?)
- Transmittals (Will a transmittal be used for a batch?)
- Prenumbering (source document or input)
- Approvals (Are approvals required for input?)

OTHER CONSIDERATIONS

- Wherever possible, provide (on the document) instructions for inputting data or completing the document.
- Keying and document preparation procedures should be consistent and predictable and should facilitate user productivity.
- Do everything possible to reduce input errors (e.g., use dashes or boxes to indicate the number of characters in a field).
- Use one form for several purposes.

Exhibit S4.5 Output Design Considerations and Guidelines

DECISIONS

- Format (e.g., 80-column report, 132-column report, preprinted form)
- Media (e.g., display screen, printout, voice, FAX)
- Output location (e.g., computer room, salesperson's laptop, point-of-sale terminal)
- Font type (e.g., serif or sans serif) and size
- Uses (e.g., to trigger some action such as in workflow systems, daily informational report, archival record, report to be annotated)
- Internal versus external users (i.e., external documents should be on preprinted forms; internal documents and reports may be in any form)
- Timeliness (e.g., on demand, daily, weekly)

CONTROLS

- Turnaround document (e.g., remittance advice attached to customer statement)
- Audit trail (e.g., sales order contains customer number)
- Control totals (provided at end of output run—e.g., hash total of customer numbers provided at end of sales order run)
- Prenumbering
- Approvals (i.e., signatures, initials, electronic signatures)
- Blind copies (e.g., blanked out quantities on the receiving department's copy of a purchase order)

OTHER CONSIDERATIONS

- Highlight important items.
- Place detail data in an appendix.
- Use summaries, a table of contents, flowcharts, and other graphics, as appropriate, to guide the user and highlight data.
- Use labels, titles, headings, and legends to help the user understand details.
- Use mnemonics to help the user retain the information.

Exhibit S4.6 summarizes some design considerations for forms. Many of the principles of good forms design can be adapted to screen design because many computer screens are really automated forms. A well-designed screen can lead to lower error rates, lower training time, lower training costs, and higher user satisfaction. Exhibit S4.7 (page 124) summarizes screen design considerations and guidelines.[8]

Prototyping is often used to develop and test user interfaces such as screens. A systems designer, using the guidelines presented here, develops a preliminary screen design. The screen design is improved as users begin to use the prototype, and it is finalized with a formal testing process.

Exhibit S4.6 Forms Design Considerations and Guidelines

FORMS TO CAPTURE DATA TO BE KEYED INTO A COMPUTER (SOURCE DOCUMENTS)

- Keep the location of fields common on all documents (e.g., document type might always be positions 1–3).
- Follow these guidelines for easy (both quick and accurate) forms completion:
  - Provide instructions on the form.
  - Minimize data to be filled in (e.g., use coding, ballots).
  - Use box format to standardize input (e.g., correct number of characters) and reduce errors made filling in the form and keying the data into the computer.
  - With box format, you can:

Provide the format: Mo   Day   Year

Provide captions: Last name   First name   M. I.

Provide ballots:

SHIP   ☐ Prepaid   ☐ Collect

- Provide for a top-to-bottom and left-to-right sequence for filling in the form.

GENERAL FORMS CONSIDERATIONS

- Will there be envelopes with mailing windows?
- Field sizes (now and future)
- Numbers/routing on form copies (e.g., accounts payable copy)
- Number of copies and paper quality (thickness)
- Can an existing form be used?
- Can forms be combined?
- Multipart sets of forms

FUNCTIONAL ASPECTS

- Through use of paper, color, and visual effects, form should generate a positive attitude.
- Terminology should be adapted to the user, who might be outside or inside the firm and trained or not trained.
- Forms leaving the organization should have a name, address, and logo.
- Include form title, number, and version number and/or date.
- Use color to increase ease of identification and use.
- Highlight with **bold**, *italic*,   , and spacing.
- Include all instructions and codes on the form (with key instructions at the top).
- Arrange items by topic or category (e.g., addresses together).
- Use one form for several purposes.

---

[8] These screen design considerations do not include the more general user interface and usability principles related to the design of other screens, such as Web sites and *decision support systems*. Rather, these considerations are restricted to screens used in the course of the processing of events-related data.

Exhibit S4.7 Screen Design Considerations and Guidelines

- If a source document is to be used, the screen and the form should be designed together to make the screen look just like the source document.
- Make screens, keying procedures, and source documents consistent across different inputs and across other screens (e.g., depressing a certain key or mouse button should always result in the same action; instructions and navigation aids are always in the same location).
- Design pages to be landscape (horizontal orientation) because most computer screens are wider than they are tall.
- Enhance speed and accuracy through use of defaults, prompting, and online help.
- Highlight text with positioning, bold face, and font size. Do not use italics, underlining, or all caps.
- Left justify (i.e., ragged right edge) to improve online reading speed.
- Acknowledge all actions. Provide a means to undo incorrect actions.
- Detect errors, identify each error, and provide an explicit error message explaining how to make corrections.
- Edit the input fields against predefined limits, against other input fields, and against stored data.
- Make screens interesting by using alignment, colors, and object sizes.
- Be consistent in form, content, and design. For example, if red is used for warning messages, do not use red for another purpose.
- Line things up exactly. Because items that break a pattern stand out, place objects out of alignment for dramatic effect.
- Minimize the amount of information on a screen. Use 25 to 30 percent of the screen area.
- Provide visual feedback. For example, use a message dialog box with a progress indicator displayed when operations are going to take longer than 7 to 10 seconds.
- Keep text clear and readable. Use concise wording of text labels, user error messages, and online help messages. Minimize the use of jargon.
- Icons and toolbars should be developed with the capability of being customized by the user.
- An icon should be designed to represent its function (e.g., scissors for "cut"). Icons should typically represent a single function.
- Choose a dominant color for an icon, bearing in mind human perception of color (e.g., red = danger and yellow = caution).
- The most frequently used menu options should be duplicated as icons on toolbars, but avoid creating long toolbars cluttered with icons.
- Only button-press or toggle-switch operations should be placed on toolbars.

Sources: Karen A. Schriver, *Dynamics in Document Design* (New York: John Wiley & Sons, Inc., 1997); Alan Cooper, *About Face: The Essentials of User Interface Design* (Forest City, CA: IDG Books Worldwide, Inc., 1995); Riki Anne Wilchins, "Screen Objects: The Building Blocks of User Interfaces," *Data Based Advisor* (August 1995): 66; Lil Mohan and John Byrne, "Designing Intuitive Icons and Toolbars," *UNIX Review* (September 1995): 49; James Hobart, "Principles of Good GUI Design," *UNIX Review* (September 1995): 37.

REVIEW QUESTIONS

RQ S4-1 What is systems implementation?

RQ S4-2 What are the systems implementation goals?

RQ S4-3 What are the three major approaches to implementing an information system?

RQ S4-4 How might an accountant participate in systems implementation?

RQ S4-5 What are the major inputs to systems implementation?

RQ S4-6 What are the items normally included in the project completion report?

RQ S4-7 What is the post-implementation review?

RQ S4-8 What are the post-implementation review goals?

RQ S4-9 What is contained in the post-implementation review report?

RQ S4-10 What is systems maintenance?

RQ S4-11 Why is the management and control of systems maintenance so important?

RQ S4-12 What are the systems maintenance goals?

RQ S4-13 What is contained in the maintenance completion report?

DISCUSSION QUESTIONS

DQ S4-1 Assume that you are the manager of an accounts receivable department. How might you be involved in system testing? Discuss fully.

DQ S4-2   a. Which, if any, category of application systems maintenance—*corrective*, *perfective*, or *adaptive*—presents the greatest risk from a *control* standpoint? Explain.

b. Which, if any, pervasive control plans from Chapter 8 in the accompanying text might be effective in controlling systems maintenance activities? What control plans other than those in Chapter 8 might be used? Discuss fully.

DQ S4-3 Give examples, other than those used in this chapter, of situations in which each of the three implementation approaches is most appropriate. Explain why that implementation approach is most appropriate.

DQ S4-4 (Appendix S4)

a. Referring to the input design considerations of Exhibit S4.4 (page 122), discuss how the *input source* might affect the design of the input. Be specific and give examples.

b. How might consideration of the source document *preparer* affect the design of the source document? Be specific and give examples.

DQ S4-5 (Appendix S4)

a. Speculate about how *color coding* of output reports or documents might be used as a control plan.

b. Speculate about how output location (see Exhibit S4.5, page 122) might be used as a control plan.

DQ S4-6 Refer to the typical contents of a project completion report. Which parts of the report would be useful in performing a post-implementation review? Discuss fully.

DQ S4-7 Using library and Internet sources, find a recent example of a systems implementation project that ran into problems. Identify what went wrong and who was responsible. With the benefit of hindsight, fully discuss what you would have done to have prevented the problems.

PROBLEMS

P S4-1 Boston Edison Company provides electric service to the residents and businesses of Boston and several other eastern Massachusetts communities.

This problem concerns the following *hypothetical* billing procedures for Boston Edison.

Field personnel take electric meter readings 10 days prior to the end of each customer's monthly billing cycle. These personnel key the meter readings into handheld units. In computer operations at the home office, the meter reading units are read by the computer, which also accesses the stored customer records and other necessary data. The quantity of kilowatts consumed and the amount due are computed, and the bill is printed (a sample bill is shown in Figure S4.6). Customers return the top half of their bills with their payments.

Because of the steady growth in the number of customers and the increased need for managerial information, Boston Edison's management has decided to upgrade its customer billing system. The new system will retain the present meter-reading procedures, but the rest of the system will be modernized. The new system should also enable managers and accountants to access customer records when desired and should provide improved information for decision making.

Required:

For each numbered item on the Boston Edison bill (Figure S4.6), indicate the immediate (versus ultimate) source of the item. For instance, the immediate source of the current meter reading would be the meter reading unit (i.e., event data), as opposed to the ultimate source, which is the meter itself. Some items may have more than one source. You have the following choices:

- C = customer records (a combination of customer and accounts receivable master data)
- CG = computer generated (such as a date or time supplied by the system)
- CC = computer calculated
- ED = event data
- CO = console operator (such as batch totals or a date to be used)

Assume that the balance (item 10) is zero (i.e., current charges and amount due are the same). Arrange your answer as follows:

Item No.	Source
1.	C
2.	?
etc.	

P S4-2 Assume that you are working with a payroll application that produces weekly paychecks, including paystubs. Following are 20 data elements that appear on the paycheck/paystub. For each numbered item, indicate the immediate (versus ultimate) source of the item. For instance, the immediate source of the number of exemptions for an employee would be the employee master data, as opposed to the ultimate source, which is the W-4 form filed by the employee. Some items may have more than one source, as in the case of item 1. You have the following choices (listed on page 128).

Figure S4.6 Boston Edison Bill to Accompany Problem S4-1

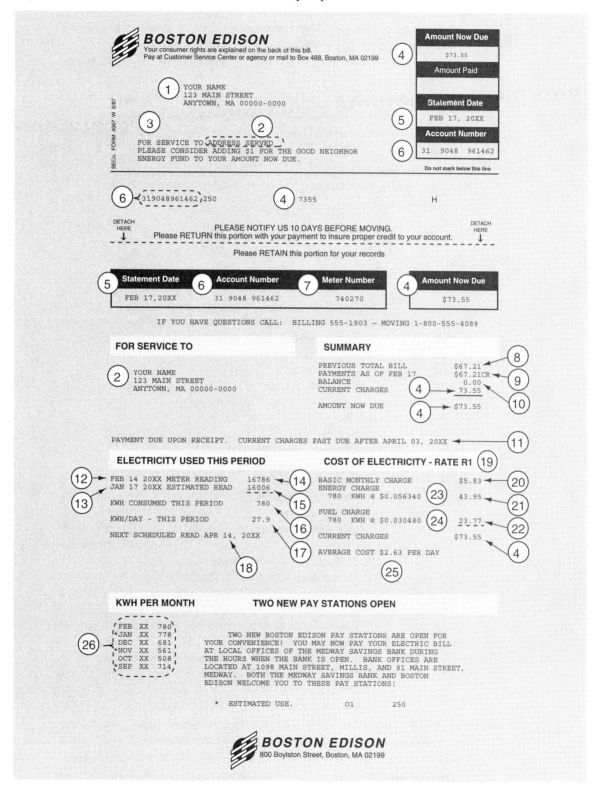

- E = employee master data
- T = time records (these are in machine-readable form and show, for each employee for each day, the time punched *in* in the morning, *out* at lunch, *in* after lunch, and *out* in the evening)
- H = table of hourly wage rates (i.e., wage rate "class" and hourly rate for each class)
- W = table of state and federal income tax withholding amounts plus FICA tax rate and annual "cutoff" amount for FICA wages
- CG = computer generated (such as a date or time of day supplied by the system)
- CC = computer calculated
- CO = console operator (such as batch totals or a date to be used)

Arrange your answer as follows:

Item No.	Source
1.	E, T
2.	?
etc.	

The items to be considered are as follows:

Number	Description
1.	Social security number
2.	Employee name
3.	Employee address
4.	Employee identification number
5.	Pay rate classification
6.	Regular hours worked
7.	Overtime hours worked
8.	Hourly pay rate
9.	Regular earnings
10.	Overtime earnings
11.	Total earnings
12.	Deduction for state income tax
13.	Deduction for FICA tax
14.	Deduction for federal income tax
15.	Union dues withheld (flat amount based on length of service)
16.	Net pay
17.	Check number (same number is also preprinted on each check form)
18.	Year-to-date amounts for items 11 through 14
19.	Pay period end date
20.	Date of check (employees are paid on Wednesday for the week ended the previous Friday)

P S4-3 Shown in Figure S4.7 is a flowchart that depicts the computer logic for updating *sequential* inventory master data for either of two types of events: goods received or goods issued.

Develop data to test the logic of the inventory update program. The test data should allow for all possible combinations of master data and event

Figure S4.7 Program Flowchart to Accompany Problem S4-3

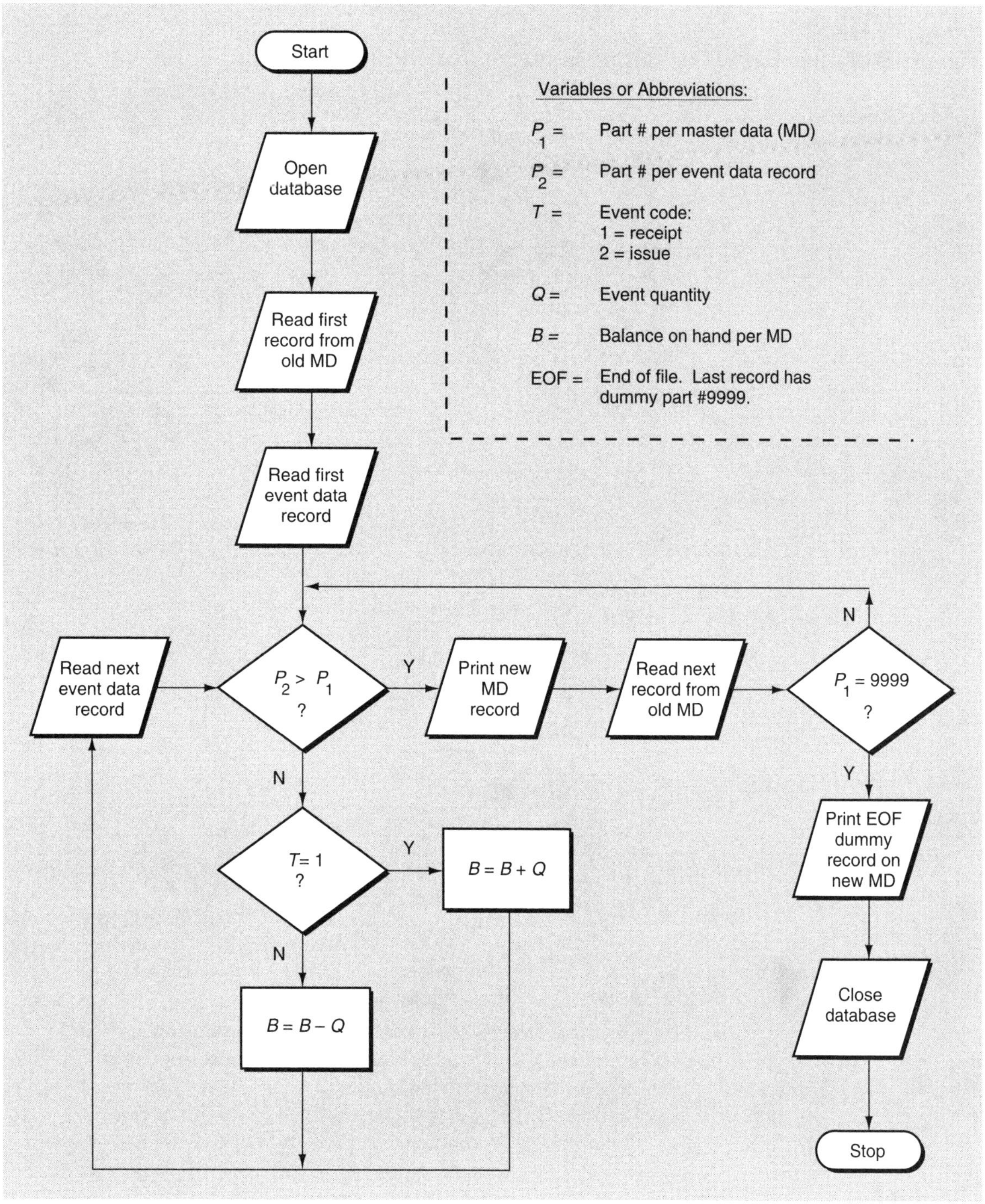

data records. *Note:* There can be more than one event for a particular part number; be sure to provide for this possibility.

P S4-4 (Appendix S4) Using the criteria presented in Appendix S4 (see Exhibits S4.4 and S4.6, pages 122 and 123, respectively), critique the bill of lading in Figure S4.8 as a form on which to capture data to be keyed into the computer.

Figure S4.8 Sample Bill of Lading to Accompany Problem S4-4

STRAIGHT BILL OF LADING—SHORT FORM—Not Negotiable—ORIGINAL

COLORADO-DENVER DELIVERY, INC.

THE MOUNTAIN MOTORWAY

Operators of DLB

SHIPPPER NO._____

DATE: _____

TO CONSIGNEE

FROM SHIPPER:

STREET

STREET

DESTINATION

ZIP CODE

ORIGIN

ZIP CODE

ROUTE

VEHICLE NUMBER

DELIVERING CARRIER

PLEASE NOTE FREIGHT CHARGES

| NO. SHIPPING UNITS | KIND OF PACKAGE, DESCRIPTION OF ARTICLES, SPECIAL MARKS, AND EXCEPTIONS | *WEIGHT SUBJECT TO CORRECTION | FOR CARRIER USE ONLY | |
| | | | RATE | EXTENSION |

CHECK BOX IF CHARGES ARE TO BE COLLECT.

Subject to Section 7 of conditions of applicable bill of lading, if the shipment is to be delivered to the consignee without recourse on the consignor, the consignor shall sign the following statement:
The carrier shall not make delivery of this shipment without payment of freight and all other lawful charges.

(Signature of Consignor)

If charges are to be prepaid, write or stamp here "To Be Prepaid"

REMIT C.O.D. TO: ADDRESS:

C.O.D. $

NOTE - WHERE THE RATE IS DEPENDENT ON VALUE, SHIPPERS ARE REQUIRED TO STATE SPECIFICALLY IN WRITING THE AGREED OR DECLARED VALUE OF THE PROPERTY.
THE AGREED OR DECLARED VALUE OF THE PROPERTY IS HEREBY SPECIFICALLY STATED BY THE SHIPPER TO BE NOT EXCEEDING:

$_____ per _____

C.O.D. FEE TO BE PAID BY
SHIPPER: _____
CONSIGNEE _____

C.O.D. FEE

TOTAL CHARGES

NOTE: UNLESS STATED ABOVE THAT CHARGES ARE TO BE PREPAID, SHIPMENT WILL MOVE FREIGHT COLLECT.

Received subject to the classifications and tariffs in effect on the date of issue of this Bill of Lading the property described in apparent good order, except as noted (contents and condition of contents of packages unknown), marked, consigned and destined as indicated above which said carrier (the word carrier being understood throughout the contract as meaning any person or corporation in possession of the property under the contract) agrees to carry to its usual place of delivery at said destination if on its route, otherwise to deliver to another carrier on the route to said destination. It is mutually agreed as to each carrier of all or any of said property over all or any portion of said route to destination, and as to each party at any time interested in all or any of said property that every service to be performed hereunder shall be subject to all the bill of lading terms and conditions in the governing classification on the date of shipment.
Shipper hereby confirms that he is familiar with all the bill of lading terms and conditions in the governing classification and the said terms and conditions are hereby agreed to by the shipper and accepted for himself and his assigns.

CHARGES ADVANCED $

EXCEPT AS SHOWN, THE AGREED VALUE ON HOUSEHOLD GOODS OR PERSONAL EFFECTS DOES NOT EXCEED 10¢ PER POUND PER ARTICLE AND THE VALUE ON PAINTINGS, PICTURES OR ARTWORK DOES NOT EXCEED 50¢ PER POUND PER ARTICLE

CARRIER

SHIPPER

PER

TOTAL PIECES:

PER

DATE

TALLY:

Source: Reprinted with permission from Colorado-Denver Delivery, Inc., Denver, CO 80217.

P S4-5 (Appendix S4) You should do this problem *only* if you have access to a computer database software package, such as Access or Oracle.

Refer to the facts in Problem S4-1, but *assume* that the Boston Edison meter readers record the meter readings on hard copy source documents instead of keying them into the portable handheld units. Then, at the home office, a data entry clerk converts the meter readings to machine-readable form by entering them into a computer.

Using the database software indicated by your instructor, apply the criteria in Appendix S4 (see Exhibit S4.7, page 124) to design an input screen for entering meter-reading event data from the manual source documents prepared by meter readers in the field. Obtain a hard copy printout of the input screen.

P S4-6 Fleet Shoe Company is having problems with its automated distribution system. The main warehouse is almost at a standstill and retailers are getting few if any Fleet shoes. Fleet had received recognition for its state-of-the-art warehouse system. However, just prior to switching to this new system, Fleet scrapped the system's software and computer hardware and adopted a new architecture. During the development there had been a high turnover of IT staff and Fleet had fired its lead systems integrator.

The new system was to automate the movement of goods in the warehouse and was to include tilting trays, conveyor belts, lifting equipment, and scanners. To operate properly, such systems require a lot of fine-tuning. The goal was to increase capacity, boost productivity, cut staff by 50 percent, and cut the time to get orders out the door to 24 hours. The software, not the hardware, seemed to be the problem. It was designed to run under UNIX but Fleet decided to use fault-tolerant computers that run a proprietary operating system. When the software vendor went out of business, they had not completed porting their software to the proprietary operating system.

Fleet's choice to replace the original platform was a computer system that itself ran warehouse management software. The new system was slower than expected. To get shoes to retailers, shoes had to be shipped directly from overseas factories and warehouses. Comments from industry specialists and consultants pointed out the chaos that resulted from the instantaneous changeover. Another speculated that Fleet did not place much importance on warehousing and rather concentrated on other aspects of its operations.

Required:

a. How would you characterize this project in terms of size, degree of definition, technical, and operational feasibilities?

b. Describe specific risks or concerns that you have for this project. Clearly explain why each is a risk or concern and the specific actions that you would recommend to mitigate the risk or concern.

P S4-7 Obtain a computer operations run manual from an actual organization. Your college or university might be a source.

Prepare a report that summarizes the contents of the run manual. Comment on the apparent reason for including each major item in the manual. If you are unsure of the reason for including certain material, interview the computer operations manager to determine the reason.

KEY TERMS

systems implementation

parallel approach

direct approach

modular approach

project completion report

computer-based training (CBT)

system test

acceptance test

operations test

environmental test

post-implementation review

post-implementation review report

systems maintenance

maintenance completion report

documents

forms

Glossary

A

Acceptance test A user-directed test of the complete system in a test environment (page 114).

Application service provider (ASP) An organization that hosts, manages, and provides access to application software and hardware over the Internet to multiple customers (page 5).

Approved configuration plan The final output of systems selection; summarizes the choices made in the selection process (page 73).

Approved systems analysis document The final output of systems analysis; contains the logical specification, physical requirements, and budget and schedule (page 48).

Approved systems design document The final deliverable of structured systems design. It documents the system design; summarizes the implementation, training, and test plans; and contains the portions of the user manual that have been developed through that point (page 89).

B

Benchmark A representative user workload, processed on each vendor's proposed system configuration, to obtain comparative throughput measures (page 81).

Business process reengineering (BPR) (Reengineering) The fundamental rethinking and radical redesign of business processes to achieve dramatic improvements in critical contemporary measures of performance, such as cost, quality, service, and speed (page 41).

C

Capability Maturity Model® (SW-CMM®) for Software A model that helps organizations evaluate the effectiveness of their software development processes and identify the key practices required to increase the maturity of those processes (page 37).

Computer-aided software engineering (CASE) The application of computer-based technology to automate the development of information systems (page 93).

Computer-based training (CBT) Provides learning via computer directly to the trainee's computer screen (page 112).

Co-sourcing *See* Outsourcing.

Cost/benefit analysis *See* Cost/benefit study.

Cost/benefit study (Cost/benefit analysis) Determines which design alternative accomplishes the user's goals for the least cost (or greatest benefit) (page 58).

Cost/effectiveness study Provides quantitative and certain qualitative information concerning alternative physical designs (page 58).

D

Deliverables Reports and other documentation that must be produced periodically during systems development to make development personnel accountable for faithful execution of systems development tasks (page 38).

Direct approach The riskiest method for systems implementation in which at time *x* the old system is stopped and the new system is begun (page 105).

Direct benefits Benefits directly attributable to the system or the system change, such as reduced personnel costs (page 59).

Direct costs Costs directly attributable to the system or the system change (page 58).

Documents (Forms) Used internally or externally to capture data that may then be input to a computer (page 121).

E

Economic feasibility A problem solution has this if the costs seem reasonable and the benefits of the solution compare favorably to competing uses for the organization's resources (page 14).

Effectiveness analysis *See* Effectiveness study.

Effectiveness study (Effectiveness analysis) Determines which alternative best accomplishes the user's goals for the system being developed (page 58).

Environmental test *See* Operations test.

External interviews Those interviews conducted with personnel outside the organization (page 82).

F

Facilities management Management by a third party of an organization's computer equipment (page 75).

Feasibility study *See* Systems survey.

Forms *See* Documents.

H

Hardware plan   Summarizes how the recommended vendor proposal will fulfill the physical requirements specified in structured systems analysis (page 87).

I

Indirect benefits   Not directly attributable to the system or the system change (page 59).

Indirect costs   Costs that are not directly attributable to the system or the system change (page 58).

Intangible benefits   Those benefits that result form having improved information, but that cannot be reasonably quantified (page 59).

Intangible cost   One that cannot be reasonably quantified, such as productivity losses caused by low employee morale (page 59).

ISO 9000-3   Documentation of standards for the processes used to develop, install, and maintain computer software (page 37).

L

Logical specification   That portion of the approved systems analysis document that describes the logic for the new system. Supporting this description are an executive summary, which is a summary of facts gathered during systems analysis including the user's requirements for the new system; the future logical and physical systems; the new system constraints; and the project leader's recommendations, approvals, and attachments (page 48).

M

Maintenance completion report   Documents the systems maintenance process; contains the change request, actions taken, recommendations for other changes, approvals (page 120).

Management control point   A place in the systems development process requiring management approval of further development work (i.e., a go/no go decision) (page 17).

Modular approach   A method for systems implementation in which the new system is either implemented one subsystem at a time or is introduced into one organizational unit at a time (page 106).

Module   A box on a structure chart representing a collection of program statements (page 91).

N

Nonrecurring costs   Costs incurred, such as those for systems development, only once to get the system operational (page 59).

O

Operational feasibility   A problem solution has this if it uses the organization's available (already possessed or obtainable) personnel and procedures (page 14).

Operations test (Environmental test)   Runs a subset of the system in the actual production environment to determine whether new equipment and other factors in the environment—such as data entry areas, document and report deliveries, telephones, and electricity—are satisfactory (page 114).

Outsourcing (Co-sourcing)   The assignment of an internal function to an outside vendor (page 4).

P

Parallel approach   A method for systems implementation in which both the old and new systems operate together for a time (page 104).

Physical requirements   That portion of the approved systems analysis document that describes the physical requirements for a new system such as required workload and volume, response times, functional layouts of reports and screens, and system growth (page 48).

Post-implementation review   An examination of a working information system, conducted soon after that system's implementation (page 116).

Post-implementation review report   Contains the post-implementation review team's conclusions and recommendations (page 118).

Preliminary feasibility study   *See* Systems survey.

Project completion report   Summarizes the implementation activities and provides documentation for operating the new system and for conducting the post-implementation review and systems maintenance (page 109).

Project plan   A statement of a project's scope, timetable, resources required to complete the project, and the project's cost (page 16).

Q

Quality assurance (QA)   Addresses the prevention and detection of errors, especially defects in software that may occur during the system development process (page 36).

R

Recurring costs   Costs incurred, such as those for equipment rental, throughout all or most of the system's life (page 59).

Reengineering   *See* Business process reengineering.

S

Service bureau   A firm providing information processing services, including hardware and software, for a fee (page 3).

Signoffs   Provided during systems development by users, managers, and auditors to signify approval of the development process and the system being developed (page 38).

Software plan   Documents how the logical specification will be implemented, using in-house development, vendor purchase or lease, ASP, or a combination of those (page 87).

Structure chart   A graphic tool for depicting the partitioning of a system into modules, the hierarchy and organization of these modules, and the communication interfaces between the modules (page 91).

Structured systems analysis   A set of procedures conducted to generate the specifications for a new (or modified) information system or subsystem (page 47).

Structured systems design   A set of procedures performed to convert the logical specification into a design that can be implemented on the organization's computer system (page 87).

System test   Verifies the new system against the original specifications (page 113).

Systems development   Comprises the steps undertaken to create or modify an organization's information system (page 36).

Systems development life cycle (SDLC) methodology   *See* Systems development methodology.

Systems development life cycle   1. A formal set of activities, or a process, used to develop and implement a new or modified information system (the systems development methodology). 2. The documentation that specifies the systems development process (the systems development standards manual). 3. The progression of information systems through the systems development process, from birth, through implementation, to ongoing use (page 36).

Systems development methodology (Systems development life cycle [SDLC] methodology)   A formalized, standardized, documented set of activities used to manage a systems development project. It should be used when information systems are developed, acquired, or maintained (page 37).

Systems implementation   A set of procedures performed to complete the design contained in the approved systems design document and to test, instill, and begin to use the new or revised information system (page 104).

Systems integrators   Consulting/systems development firms that develop systems under contract (page 4).

Systems maintenance   The modification (e.g., repair, correction, enhancement) of existing applications (page 119).

Systems selection   A set of procedures performed to choose the computer software and hardware for an information system (page 70).

Systems survey (Feasibility study, Preliminary feasibility study)   A set of procedures conducted to determine the feasibility of a potential systems development project and to prepare a systems development plan for projects considered feasible (page 45).

T

Tangible benefits   Those benefits that can be reasonably quantified (page 59).

Tangible cost   One that can be reasonably quantified, such as personnel costs (page 59).

Technical feasibility   A problem solution has this if it uses available (already possessed or obtainable) hardware and software technology (page 14).

Throughput   Quantity of work performed in a period of time (page 79).

Turnkey system   A system in which a supplier has purchased computer hardware and has developed or acquired software to put together a computer system to be sold to end users (page 3).

V

Validate   To determine whether a system meets the requirements of the RFP (page 79).

Index

A

Acceptance test, *def.*, 114
Accounting information system (AIS), acquiring from external parties, 5–6
Accounting information system (AIS) acquisition
accountant's involvement in, 6–10
achieving objectives of, 10–11
Accounting information system (AIS) acquisition cycle
illus., 7
phases, purposes, and tasks, 8
project management, 11–12
Accounting information system (AIS) analysis
needs analysis, 17–24
preliminary survey, 12–17
Accounting information system (AIS) selection, 24–29
determining final solution, 27–29
evaluating feasible solutions, 24–27
AIS, *See* Accounting information system
Application service provider (AP), *def.*, 5
Approved configuration plan, *def.*, 73
Approved feasibility document, contents of, 18
Approved systems analysis document
completing and packaging, 60–61
contents of, 50
def., 48
Approved systems design document, 89–91; *def.*, 89

B

Benchmark, *def.*, 81
Benefits
direct, 59
indirect, 59
intangible, 59
tangible, 59
Business process reengineering (BPR), 40–42
def., 41
making success of, 43

C

Capability Maturity Model® (SW-CMM®) for Software
def., 37
five maturity levels of, 38
Change management, 42–43
Computer-aided software engineering (CASE), 93–94; *def.*, 94
Computer-based training (CBT), *def.*, 112
Co-sourcing, *def.*, 4
Cost/benefit analysis, *def.*, 58
Cost/benefit study, *def.*, 58
Cost/effectiveness study, *def.*, 58
Costs
direct, 58
indirect, 58
intangible, 59
nonrecurring, 59
recurring, 59
tangible, 59

D

Deliverables, *def.*, 38
Direct approach, *def.*, 105
Direct benefits, *def.*, 59
Direct costs, *def.*, 58
Documents, *def.*, 121

E

Economic feasibility, *def.*, 14
Effectiveness analysis, *def.*, 58
Effectiveness study, *def.*, 58
Environmental test, *def.*, 114
External interviews, *def.*, 82

F

Facilities management, *def.*, 75
Feasibility
economic, 14
operational, 14
technical, 14
Feasibility document, contents of, 18
Feasibility study, 14; *def.*, 45
Feasible solutions
determining, 26
evaluating, 24–26
Forms, *def.*, 121
Forms design, considerations and guidelines, 123

H

Hardware acquisition
alternatives, 74–76
external, 74–75
financing alternatives, 75–76
internal, 74
Hardware plan, *def.*, 87

I

Implementation plan and budget, developing, 92
Implementation test plan, developing, 92
Indirect benefits, *def.*, 59
Indirect costs, *def.*, 58
Information systems development phases, purposes, and tasks, 40
Input design, considerations and guidelines, 122
Intangible benefits, *def.*, 59
Intangible cost, *def.*, 59
Interviews, external, 82
ISO 9000-3, *def.*, 37

L

Logical specification, *def.*, 48
Logical system, defining future, 52–56

M

Maintenance completion report
contents of, 120
def., 120
Management control plan, *def.*, 17
Modular approach, *def.*, 106
Module
def., 91
specifying in systems design, 91–92

N

Needs analysis, 17–24
Nonrecurring costs, *def.*, 59

O

Operational feasibility, *def.*, 14
Operations test, *def.*, 114
Output design, considerations and guidelines, 122
Outsourcing, *def.*, 4

P

Parallel approach, *def.*, 104
Physical requirements, *def.*, 48
Physical system
designing alternative future, 56–58
selecting best alternative, 58–60
studying and documenting current, 51
Plan
approved configuration, 73
configuration, 86–87
hardware, 87
management control, 17
project, 14–16
software, 87
Post-implementation review, 116–120; *def.*, 116
Post-implementation review report
contents of, 118
def., 118
Preliminary feasibility study, 14; *def.*, 45
Preliminary survey, 12–17
Project completion report, *def.*, 109
Project management, 11–12
Project plan, 14–16; *def.*, 16

Q

Quality assurance (QA), 36–37; *def.*, 36

R

Recurring costs, *def.*, 59
Request for proposal
contents of, 28
preparing, 77–78

S

Screen design, considerations and guidelines, 124
Service bureau, *def.*, 3
Signoffs, *def.*, 38
Software plan, *def.*, 87
Structure chart, *def.*, 91
Structured systems analysis, 47–61; *def.*, 47; *See also* Systems analysis
Structured systems design
def., 87

tasks and documents, *illus.,*
90
See also Systems design
Systems analysis
definition and goals, 47–48
structured, 47–61
tasks and documents, 48–61
triggering, 48–51
Systems design
accountant's involvement in,
89
completing document, 93
definition and goals, 87–89
implementation plan and
budget, 92
implementation test plan, 92
intermediate steps in, 91–93
modules, 91–92
structured, 87
tasks in, 89
training program, 92
triggering, 91
user manual, 92
Systems design deliverable,
89–91
Systems development
accountant's involvement in,
44
def., 36
Systems development life cycle,
def., 36

Systems development life cycle
(SDLC) methodology, *def.,*
37
Systems development
methodology
characteristics of, 38
def., 37
Systems development process
controlling, 36–40
methodology, 37–40
quality assurance, 36–37
Systems implementation
accountant's involvement in,
106–109
approaches to, 104–106
completing design, 110
computer programs,
111–112
conversion, 115–116
def., 104
direct approach, 105
hardware and software,
110–111
intermediate steps, 110–
116
modular approach, 106
obtaining approvals, 115
parallel approach, 104
personnel, 112–113
project completion report,
109

tasks and documents, *illus.,*
108
testing system, 113–115
triggering, 109
user manual, 113
Systems implementation deliverable, 109
Systems implementation plans,
106
Systems integrators
def., 4
guidelines for use of, 5
Systems maintenance,
119–120; *def.,* 119
Systems operation, 116–120
post-implementation review,
116–119
systems maintenance,
119–120
Systems selection
accountant's involvement in,
72–73
configuration plan, 86–87
def., 70
intermediate steps in, 76–
87
requests for proposals,
77–78
software plan, 83–86
tasks and documents, *illus.,*
76

triggering, 73
vendor proposals, 78–83
Systems selection deliverable,
73
Systems survey, 44–47
def., 45
definition and goals, 45
tasks and documents, 45–47

T

Tangible benefits, *def.,* 59
Tangible cost, *def.,* 59
Technical feasibility, *def.,* 14
Throughput, *def.,* 79
Training program, developing,
92
Turnkey system, *def.,* 3

U

User manual, developing, 92

V

Validate, *def.,* 79
Vendor information, sources
of, 78
Vendor proposals, evaluating,
78–83